Contents

Preface

The beautiful and lovely mystery of the holy Trinity has intrigued the minds of the wisest scholars throughout the history of the Christian church. Volumes have been written concerning the personalities and primary ministries of the various members of the Godhead—Father, Son, and Holy Spirit.

Fortunately, one does not have to be a trained theologian to encounter the love of God as it reaches out to us through all the marvelous ministries of the matchless Trinity. One often hears people refer to their relationship with the Father, or the Son, or the Holy Spirit in most intimate and affectionate ways—obviously born out of personal experience. Expressions of endearment such as: "My dear heavenly Father," "Beloved Lord Jesus," or "My Blessed Comforter," all speak of warm and meaningful relationships with the various members of the triune Godhead.

Still many Christians have a limited appreciation of God because only one or two personalities of the Trinity have been emphasized in their experience. I know there has been a progressive realization of the Godhead in my own life, and I have discovered a similar pattern in the experience of

Our Heavenly Father

by Robert Frost

LOGOS INTERNATIONAL
Plainfield, New Jersey

OUR HEAVENLY FATHER
Copyright © 1978 by Logos International. All Rights Reserved.
International Standard Book Number: 0-88270-266-1
Library of Congress Catalog Card Number: 77-95141
Logos International, Plainfield, New Jersey 07060
Printed in the United States of America

others. After committing my life to Jesus Christ as my Lord and Savior, I wanted to get better acquainted with Him in every way I knew how. There is something very appealing about Jesus that draws our lives to Him in a close bond of love. The centrality and supremacy of the Lord Jesus Christ becomes the integrating theme which gathers and relates all of creation into God's eternal plan and purpose.

I soon discovered, however, it was one thing to recognize Jesus as the center of divine purpose, but quite another to possess the power to fulfill that purpose. It was this need in my life which brought me into a personal encounter with the person of the Holy Spirit as the source of that power which can enable us to express the life of Jesus Christ in a practical way. Some have referred to the Holy Spirit as the least known member of the Godhead. Certainly there was much I wanted to learn and experience concerning His gracious ministry with regard to Christ Jesus. I discovered it was His desire to reveal Jesus to us, realize Jesus in us, release Jesus through us, and finally to relate us all to one another in Him.

My wife and I entered into the Spirit-filled life in 1955. Since that time there have been many opportunities to share our experience in the Holy Spirit with those of God's people who likewise have longed for this missing dimension in their lives. Indeed, there has been a worldwide move of the Holy Spirit throughout Christendom during the last decade and a half which is still rapidly growing in its influence.

One mark of the Spirit-baptized Christian is his desire to relate his life to the ultimate purpose of his heavenly Father for this hour in history. There is an awareness of divine destiny which constrains us to be about our Father's business. God is uniting His people for a glorious and powerful end-time witness to the world. The body of Christ, however, will only be as strong and steady as is its component members. It is for this reason that a personal appreciation concerning the fulness of the Godhead is imperative for each individual Christian.

I came to realize in my own experience that I had a very faulty concept concerning the fatherhood of God which was limiting the power of the Holy Spirit through my life. There were hurts that needed to be healed, and a renewed understanding of my position as a son in His family. Consequently, for the last few years I have been in the process of becoming better acquainted with my heavenly Father. I have found the same need and heart-cry wherever we have gone in our travels throughout the world. Truly, our heavenly Father desires that His children find the strength and security which only His love can bring. I am convinced that this is one of the great but hidden needs within the body of Christ. Divine sonship and daughterhood rest full-weight upon a genuine heart-knowledge of the Father's love.

Recently while visiting a mountain community here on the West Coast, we were particularly blessed when one of the Spirit-filled residents shared with us a beautiful revelation from the Lord in which it was as if the Father himself spoke these words: "Tell my people that I love them; tell them that I care." There had been a corresponding echo in my own heart for some time which arose from a teaching series on the fatherhood of God given at conferences both here and abroad. The depth of response and personal encouragement regarding this important theme became the inspiration for writing this book.

1

Fatherhood:
The Foundation for Life

"What is a father, anyway? I haven't the slightest idea of what a father is supposed to be, say, or do. The fatherhood of God is a meaningless concept as far as I am concerned."

These were the words of a young lady in her early twenties; they were said with pathetic sincerity. I had just finished my first session in a series on the fatherhood of God, and had felt my carefully planned introduction had been well received. I began to have second thoughts, however, as our conversation continued, and I realized that much of what I had said about our heavenly Father held very little meaning for this beloved daughter of God. Words had reached her mind, but there was no response at the level of her heart, for this part of her emotional life had never developed. She had never known the love of an earthly father, and consequently had no familiar reference with which to appreciate the love of her heavenly Father. For her the whole idea of fatherhood was a total mystery.

We were created to be loved by our Father God, and to return that love to Him and share it with others. Life without God's love isn't life at all, but only an existence without eternal purpose. No wonder this young lady was prompted to pursue the hope which was planted in her heart during the teaching session. Her questions were not challenging, but searching—as if she were on the threshold of discovering something which had been missing all of her life. What a privilege it was to be a part of that discovery with her.

What Is a Father Anyway?

The question concerning the character of fatherhood is a good one. Just what is a father? I turned the thought over in my mind repeatedly as I revised my second teaching session scheduled for the next day. I had never been faced with that question in such a direct manner before. It deserved and demanded an appropriate answer.

The Holy Scriptures portray a warm and personal picture of fatherhood as characterized by God himself. Let us consider some of the more important roles related to the father-image.

Creator: One who imparts life after his own nature to his beloved children.

> For in him we live, and move, and have our being
> . . . For we are also his offspring. (Acts 17:28)

Protector: One who in love protects, guards, defends and shields his children from harm.

> How precious is thy steadfast love, O God! The children of men take refuge in the shadow of thy wings. (Ps. 36:7, RSV)

Provider: One who lovingly anticipates and provides for his children's every need.

> Therefore take no thought, saying, What shall we eat? or, What shall we drink? or, Wherewithal shall we be clothed? . . . For your heavenly Father knoweth that ye have need of all of these things. (Matt. 6:31-32)

Instructor: One who guides, directs, and instructs the lives of his children for their greatest good.

> Hear, O sons, a father's instruction, and be attentive, that you may gain insight. (Prov. 4:1, RSV)
> I will instruct thee and teach thee in the way which thou shalt go: I will guide thee with mine eye. (Ps. 32:8)

Corrector: One who takes time to correct and discipline his children because he loves them.

> My son, do not despise the Lord's discipline or be weary of his reproof, for the Lord reproves him whom he loves, as a father the son in whom he delights. (Prov. 3:11-12, RSV)

Redeemer: One who forgives his children's faults and failures and lovingly seeks to redeem their lives whatever the cost.

> The Lord is merciful and gracious, slow to anger and abounding in steadfast love. As far as the east is from the west, so far does he remove our transgressions from us. As a father pities his children, so the Lord pities those who fear him. (Ps. 103:8, 12-13, RSV)

Comforter: One who comforts and consoles his beloved children that they may be encouraged to move forward in faith.

> Blessed be the God and Father of Our Lord Jesus Christ, the Father of mercies and God of all comfort, who comforts us in all our affliction, so that we may be able to comfort those who are in any affliction, with the comfort with which we ourselves are comforted by God. (2 Cor. 1:3-4, RSV)

From this scriptural sketch we discover that all of the functions of fatherhood are based upon a personal relationship of love. To the extent that love is lacking, there will be a serious limitation in emotional development. The same principle applies on the heavenly level. To be unaware that we are truly beloved sons and daughters will seriously affect our spiritual development.

Love: The Key to Perfect Sonship and Daughterhood

The fatherhood of God presumes a beloved sonship and daughterhood with all the privileges and responsibilities of divine family life as perfectly and beautifully portrayed by our elder and model Brother, Jesus Christ. Satan's most subtle and sinister scheme for frustrating the Father's plan for our lives is to deceive us concerning the power and purpose of God's love for us. It all began with the first family when in the guise of a graceful serpent, the deceiver convinced Adam and Eve that "true love" would never place any restrictions upon its recipients. They succumbed to the temptation to seek their own pleasure rather than that of their Father-Creator, whose love had been brought into question. Their doubt led to disobedience, which in turn

4

produced death—a familiar pattern which has perpetrated itself throughout the history of mankind.

As summarized and illustrated in the diagram below, Satan ever seeks to deceive us concerning the truth about the love of our heavenly Father and thereby limit our life in His family.

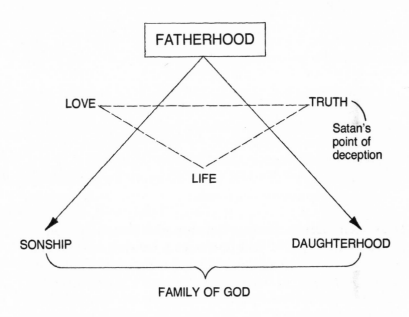

Love: The True Ground for Faith and Obedience

The basic importance of the love principle is impressed upon us in a rather vivid way in Scripture. Jesus said that in our time of thirst, we could come to Him and drink, and if we would continue to believe in Him as the Scriptures have said, out of our innermost being would flow rivers of living water. John in his Gospel interprets this passage as a beautiful picture of the Spirit-filled life (John 7:37-39). Our responsibility is to come in obedience and drink in faith, and from the fountain of our life the various streams of the Spirit will freely flow. This obviously refers to the many manifestations of the Holy Spirit—the fruit and gifts of the Spirit—which enable us to express the life of Christ. Only doubt and disobedience can stem the tide of this rising river of life from God.

In other words, to change the metaphor, our Christian walk is dependent upon the two basic steps of faith and obedience. One is reminded of the familiar words in the hymn by Daniel B. Towner: "There is no other way to be happy in Jesus than to trust and obey." We are delighted to discover that our walk in the Spirit can be reduced to these two simple steps. Here is the obvious key to the victorious Christian life. The secret to spiritual success is summed up in the simple little phrase—trust and obey.

Our enthusiasm is short-lived, however, for little words can represent a great responsibility in personal experience. It is very easy to talk and even sing about faith and obedience, but quite another matter to put the principles into practice in our daily lives. We may arise with great intentions for a glorious day with God only to find our enthusiasm and performance noticeably dims when the children get up, for we face some earthy situation at school, work, or in our Christian community. We sadly discover that unexpected pressures or demands can quickly crowd us into the parallel ditches of doubt or disobedience if there is no basic motivation which supports and sustains our daily walk with Christ.

Sometime ago while holding this problem before the Lord, I was reminded that it takes more than two feet to walk. Our astronauts high in the heavens each had two good feet, but could not walk from one compartment of their spaceship to another. The reason, of course, was simple: They were

6

beyond the earthly pull of gravity, and it was impossible for them to place their feet upon the floor. In order to walk, our feet must arise from and rest upon the ground of our pathway.

It now becomes clear that there is something more basic than faith and obedience in our Christian walk. What is the "ground" from which and upon which the steps of faith and obedience arise and rest? It is the love and truth of God. Our heavenly Father is not only loving and truthful; He is love, and He is truth. This is His nature; He is both wise and affectionate.

Divine Love and Truth Are Inseparable

Our heavenly Father always communicates His truth in love, and His love with truth. Never are the two separated from one another. This is an important concept, because man may separate his knowledge about the truth from God's love and merely minister in a mental sort of way. Knowledge apart from the Spirit of love, however, will never impart life. In fact, we can wield our knowledge like a sword and actually wound or destroy a weakened brother or sister in Christ. It is possible for us to be dead right, or as a friend of mine used to say, "We can be so right we are wrong!"

All of us probably have been on the receiving end of ministry which has lacked the love and compassion we desperately needed. Instead of sympathetic words of counsel and comfort, we received a lecture or a couple of computerized Bible promises which actually left us with a heavier spirit. We may even wonder if such a heartless attitude is that of our heavenly Father as well. If someone implies they are ministering in the name of the Lord, it is easy to assume their lack of sympathetic understanding is a reflection of Him.

The Lord dealt with me rather directly about the

necessity of ministering His truth in love some years ago. An elderly woman in my Bible class was having family problems, and I had counseled and prayed with her on several occasions. After some weeks, she again approached me after class concerning her family situation. I was tired, irritated, and a little annoyed that she couldn't handle some of her own problems—especially after her sitting under *my* teaching for weeks. I impatiently quoted a couple of Scripture verses on faith, and was about to turn away, when she collapsed at my feet. I realized then that she was at an emotional breaking point, and I had been too insensitive to recognize how desperate her condition was.

I discovered one can do a great deal of repenting in the time it takes to reach a kneeling position. Two ladies joined me in ministry as we instructed our dear sister to rest and be at peace, while we prayed that the Lord would renew her strength and restore her faith. We, in effect, gave her a transfusion of God's love, and after a few minutes, she arose obviously transformed by the power of God's Spirit. The greater transformation, however, occurred, I believe, in my own heart, because I realized as never before the importance of "speaking the truth in love" (Eph. 4:15).

The same principle applies in ministering God's love; it can never be separated from His truth. However, it is possible for us to minister in a sentimental way from our feelings about God's love, yet be apart from His truth. We may feel sorry for someone's sad plight (perhaps of their own making) and tell them what they want to hear rather than what they need to hear. Actually, we only succeed in deepening their pit of pity, and may even discover we have joined them in their depths of despair!

A middle-aged lady shared with me the tragic turn of events which had changed her entire life. Her husband, a clergyman, had left her without support to marry a younger woman who was closely related to the immediate family. The only opportunity to visit her grandchildren involved repeated exposure to the whole wretched affair. In describing God's grace and provision throughout the entire ordeal, she would brighten, and the power of praise would elevate her spirit. Just as quickly her face would fall, however, as she repeatedly related the humiliation, insecurity, and pain she had experienced as a result of her personal tragedy.

I sought to have a sensitive spirit both to her heart-cry and to God's Word that I might minister His love in truth. Something more than sympathy was needed. To my dismay the words self-pity were repeatedly impressed upon my heart and mind. I argued with God that I couldn't inform her of such a weakness in her life, and run the risk of adding another burden to a soul already weary and wounded by grief. After some time, I finally agreed to obey, but only if the Holy Spirit would enable me to minister His love with truth and understanding.

God graciously responded, and I began by sincerely sympathizing with her in her tragic plight. I told her that if ever there was a woman who in the natural had the right to feel sorry for herself and engage in self-pity, undoubtedly she was that person. I then shared with her that God had impressed me that this, however, was a serious defect in her spiritual armor which allowed the adversary to penetrate her soul with darkness and despair. It was his design to wound, weaken, and totally destroy her life if possible. Her heavenly Father, however, was aware that one of His dearest daughters needed His loving help, healing, and protection. That was the reason her expressions of thanksgiving brought such obvious blessing to her heart and mind; it was the Lord's special and personal ministry to her as a beloved child of God. Furthermore, as she leaned upon

His faithfulness, the Lord was going to enlarge her ministry to the young girls in her dormitory where she was currently engaged as a housemother.

She gratefully received the word of truth because it had been warmly motivated by God's restoring love. Her Father wanted her to know that He cared for her very much, and desired to make up for the loss in her earthly family by giving her a larger place in His heavenly family. Again we discover how graciously God apportions both His love and truth that we might experience His healing power.

Love and Truth Provide the Motivation and Direction for Our Walk of Faith and Obedience

Yes, the Word of the Lord is a beautiful balance of both truth and love. There is a reason for this: Divine love provides the motivation for our faith and obedience, while divine truth provides the direction they are to take. This is true in a limited way in our natural relationships with one another. We trust those whom we feel love us without reservation. I would trust my wife with my life because I know she loves me deeply. There have been times I have disappointed, failed, and even hurt her, but it has never turned off her love for me. We learn to trust those who truly love us "for better or for worse."

Furthermore, we wish to respond to those who love us so faithfully. We basically want to please them and fulfill their desires. We have even coined the little phrase, "your slightest wish is my command." Love seeks out the will and pleasure of the beloved.

> If ye love me, keep my commandments. (John 14:15)
> For this is the love of God, that we keep his commandments: and his commandments are not

grievous. (1 John 5:3)

Why do we obey the Lord? Because we have to? Because we will be punished if we don't? No. It is because we love Him and want to please someone who has proven that He truly loves us without reservation.

> When we were utterly helpless with no way of escape, Christ came at just the right time and died for us sinners. Now it is an extraordinary thing for one to give his life even for an upright man, though once in a while a man is brave enough to die for a generous friend. But the proof of God's amazing love is this: that it was while we were yet sinners that Christ died for us. (Rom. 5:6-8, various versions)

Apart from the truth about God's love, our trust and obedience is going to be a forced affair which eventually will leave us weary, worn, and under condemnation for failing to measure up to divine expectation. Indeed, if we are not motivated by love, we will be motivated by fear and a heavy sense of obligation which effectively rob us of our joy and peace in the Lord.
Faith which does not arise from an awareness of God's love and gracious will for our lives will become a cerebral exercise wherein we strive to work up our confidence. How many times I have tried to force my faith by mentally trying to believe in the face of contrary circumstances. It is easy to slip into the error of putting more faith in our faith or in our prayer than in Christ, who is the author and finisher of our faith and the one to whom we are praying. Such endeavors are always characterized by a certain amount of stress and strain, coupled with a hidden fear that our faith isn't strong

enough, or that our prayer isn't long enough to reach the ear of God. There is then the tendency to make up for our lack of devotion by a peculiar combination of commotion and emotion. I have found prayers tend to become louder and longer than necessary under such circumstances, and a tension can develop which signals our departure from the simplicity of childlike faith. We may even be tempted to use God's promises as a lever to force His power in the direction of our problem, not realizing His will for our lives involves a harmony of time, place, people, motive, means, and loving purpose.

I recall years ago repeatedly praying for our preschool daughter who was suffering from a midnight earache. After several excursions to her room for additional prayers, my self-image as a man of faith began to crumble. In my frustration and resentment, I finally decided I would put God on the spot, and instructed my daughter to pray for her own healing. There was still no relief, and I realized I wasn't going to have a triumphant testimony for our next prayer meeting.

I had recalled earlier in the ordeal that my wife, who is a nurse, had brought home a sample bottle of ear drops. I finally resorted to the medication, and our daughter immediately went to sleep and was fine in the morning. Throughout the entire episode I was so busy trying to generate a powerful prayer in faith, I failed to appreciate the loving provision of God which He had anticipated months earlier. Basically my problem was derived from a misconception concerning the loving nature and character of our heavenly Father, and the variety of ways which He utilizes in meeting our needs.

Obedience: Forced by Fear or Motivated by Love?

The same kind of problem can arise concerning the

question of obedience. If we endeavor to obey God for any reason or from any motive outside of His divine purpose and love, we will find ourselves continually living under a cloud of fear and frustration. Our so-called "walk in the Spirit" will seemingly degenerate into a "forced march" directed by a divine dictator. Satan thus seeks to pervert the beautiful principle of obedience and thereby limit its power to bring release to our lives.

One of my students approached me following a class in a Christian college where I was teaching. She was obviously very disturbed concerning the will of God for an important decision which she felt she faced. The students had been given the opportunity to contribute to the purchase of some needed classroom chairs, and she was experiencing intense inner conflict regarding whether she should give, and if so, how much. Her finances were limited, yet she didn't want to miss God's will concerning her life of faith and obedience.

Such opportunities often provide people with the wholesome privilege of expressing their love, and exercising their faith. However, she seemed so concerned that I sensed more of a compelling spirit of fear rather than an attitude of loving obedience. In the course of our conversation she mentioned how she had given to a similar project a week or so earlier, and was torn with indecision regarding the present challenge. It then became clear that she had brought herself under a bondage which God had never intended. She was laboring under a misconception concerning the character of her heavenly Father. With great feeling and spiritual conviction I assured her that God was far more concerned about her as His beloved daughter than He was in what she was doing for Him. He wanted her relationship with Him to be based on His love rather than her fear.

There is a godly fear, but its purpose is to protect and purify our life and love relationship with the Lord, not to bring us into condemnation and bondage. She left with joy in her heart and praise on her lips for the renewed assurance of God's love. Obedience was not her problem, but rather a mistaken idea of divine fatherhood. Again we see how essential it is that our walk of faith and obedience be firmly placed upon the ground of God's truth and love.

The various aspects of our life and walk in the Spirit as previously discussed are summarized in the following diagram:

OUR SPIRITUAL WALK

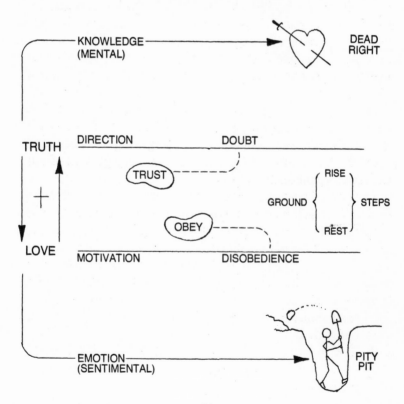

Threefold Basis for Satanic Deception

Jesus referred to the devil as a liar and the father of lies (John 8:44). We have already mentioned his deceptive ways in regard to the temptation of Adam and Eve in the Garden of Eden. The Apostle Paul rather pointedly refers to this incident in his second letter to the Corinthian church:

> But now I am afraid that as the serpent deceived Eve by his cunning, so your minds may be seduced from a sincere and pure devotion to Christ. (2 Cor. 11:3, various versions)

It comes as no surprise, therefore, to discover that our adversary will seek to deceive us concerning the truth about the character of our loving heavenly Father. As we have seen, a faulty concept of God's love will weaken our walk of faith and obedience, and thereby limit our life in the Lord. Such deception is the most devastating weapon that Satan could devise to effectively strike at the very ground of our Christian experience.

How will the devil endeavor to deceive the children of God? What is his strategy and means of operation? The answer can be found in his threefold plan for deception, which is diagramed on the following page:

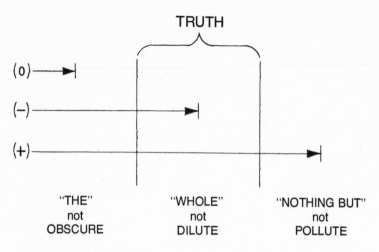

In our courts of law we swear to tell:
1. The truth—nothing concealed (obscured).
2. The whole truth—nothing left out (diluted).
3. Nothing but the truth—nothing added (polluted).

Such a statement has been carefully designed to avoid a testimony of deception. Satan utilizes these same three principles of deception to create within our minds a faulty concept concerning the character of our heavenly Father. He will keep us totally ignorant of God's love if he can. Otherwise, he will seek to limit our understanding of that love, or qualify it by adding something that pollutes the purity of that love.

A Misconception of God's Love

Some picture the love of God as a kind of permissive sentimentality which would never confront man with his sin or the consequences of that sin. In fact, sin is not defined as man's unrighteousness and rebellion for which he is responsible, but only his ignorance of the divine light of God's love and truth which is merely waiting within his heart to be fanned into flame by an awareness of his own self-potential. Furthermore, it is inconceivable that a God of love would ever send anyone to hell as a consequence of his self-willed sin. Hell is limited to this life only and is merely the pain and difficulty which is experienced as a consequence of not realizing the harmony of divine life which lies dormant within each human heart. There is no judgment after death, for at that time, regardless of the kind of life lived on earth, all will immediately see the error of earthly illusions and enter into the bliss of divine light and love. Of course, the existence of a personal devil or demons is denied, because a loving God would never be responsible for the creation of such evil beings. God is portrayed as an indulgent and condescending father-figure who will never hold man accountable for his evil ways since they are a result of his ignorance, for which he is not responsible.

Obviously, to emphasize God's love in such a soft and sentimental way is to ignore His holiness, righteousness, and justice. If man is totally relieved of any sense of moral responsibility, he is also deprived of the dignity of individual decision, which is one aspect of being created in God's image. God is sovereign, and a measure of sovereignty (freedom of will) was given to man, for which he is held accountable. Love, loyalty, and worship by their nature require a freedom of personal choice. All three lose their meaning if forced or automatically programed. Divine love without human responsibility is a deception based on a half-truth.

A Misconception of God's Justice

On the other extreme, the justice and wrath of God regarding evil can be twisted to such an extent that the features of a merciful heavenly Father are distorted in a most fearful fashion. The severity of God has been most vividly depicted in the imaginations of some rather notable preachers and scholars:

> When thou diest, thy soul will be tormented alone; that will be a hell for it: but at the Day of Judgement, thy body will join thy soul, and then thou wilt have twin Hells, thy soul sweating drops of blood, and thy body suffused with agony. In fire, exactly like that we have on earth, thy body will lie, asbestos like, forever unconsumed, all thy veins roads for the feet of pain to travel on, every nerve a string, on which the Devil shall forever play his diabolical tune of Hell's unutterable lament.
>
> —*Rev. C.H. Spurgeon*
>
> In order that nothing be wanting to the happiness of the blessed in heaven, a perfect view is granted them of the tortures of the damned.
>
> —*Thomas Aquinas*
>
> The sight of hell's torments will exalt the happiness of the saints forever; it will give them a more lively relish.
>
> —*Jonathan Edwards*

Such an unscriptural perversion of God's character leaves one with an inner sense of revulsion.

Even the standards of earthly fatherhood would be violated by such a fiendish description of retaliatory behavior and meaningless torture. Some years ago, a West Coast newspaper printed the following Associated Press report:

> A "Father's Curse" was the legacy left by ———, member of a well known family here, to his two

daughters by a former wife, in a will filed for probate in Superior Court. "And to my two daughters, ——— and ———, he wrote in his own hand, "by virtue of their unfilial attitude toward a doting father, and because they have repeatedly thwarted my efforts to see them, I leave the sum of one dollar each and a father's curse. May their respective lives be fraught with misery, unhappiness, and poignant sorrow. May their deaths be soon and of a lingering, malign, and torturous nature. May their souls rest in hell and suffer the torments of the damned for eternity."

Obviously such an attitude is not that of a true father, but of a devilish fiend seeking the satisfaction of personal revenge. Yet this is the very picture which many have of God the Father.

The Threefold Basis for a Faulty Concept of Our Heavenly Father

What is our heavenly Father really like? Why do so many sincere and dedicated Christians have such a distorted concept of God the Father? How has Satan succeeded in deceiving so many people concerning the true nature of God's love, thereby undermining their life of faith and obedience?

The answers to such questions appear to be related to three basic causes:

1. Certain legalistic extremes in Western theology which present God primarily as a merciless judge rather than a loving Father-Redeemer.
2. Faulty earthly father relationships which

19

grossly distort the true image of fatherhood.
3. Personal misfortunes which seem difficult to reconcile with the love of an all-powerful Father-God.

We shall seek to consider each of these three themes in the chapters to follow, and allow both God's Spirit and God's Word to enlighten our minds and open our hearts concerning the true character of our loving heavenly Father.

2

The Fatherhood of God in the Gospels

A systematic study of the fatherhood of God throughout Scripture reveals a progressive unfolding of the concept as one proceeds through the Old Testament writers to those of the New Testament gospels and epistles. Such a survey will help us to better understand the thinking of the early church. We then can trace traditional shifts in attitude throughout church history concerning the character of God which carry over into modern-day theology. We shall make some very interesting and revealing discoveries.

Old Testament Concepts Concerning the Fatherhood of God

There are relatively few references in the Old Testament to the fatherhood of God except in a general creative or theocratic sense. God was readily recognized as the Father-Creator of all things, including man. Malachi, the prophet, expresses this thought rather directly:

Have we not all one father? Has not one God created us? (Mal. 2:10, RSV)

The children of Israel also believed that they were a chosen people related to God and each other by a special covenant relationship which gave them a peculiar identity among the pagan nations. As author of that covenant, God was recognized as the divine patriarch of their national family.

> Wherefore David blessed the Lord before all the congregation: and David said, Blessed be thou, Lord God of Israel our father, forever and ever. (1 Chron. 29:10)

For the most part, however, the idea of God as a heavenly Father was rather general and impersonal. In a collective sense He was their Father-Creator, and the Father of their nation, but the feeling of a warm personal relationship as an individual son or daughter was lacking. This was to wait for the coming of Christ who would personally reveal the special relationship each individual could have with his heavenly Father.

I can't help but feel, however, that some of the Old Testament prophets and writers must have had glimpses of their relationship with God as beloved sons and daughters. They lived in a patriarchal society where warm, intimate expressions of family love were commonplace. It is difficult to think that some of them would not project this personal love relationship towards God. Perhaps the Psalmist gives us some supporting reason for our thought:

> Father of the fatherless and protector of widows is God in his holy habitation. (Ps. 68:5, RSV)
> As a father pities his children, so the Lord pities those who fear him. (Ps. 103:13, RSV)

Nevertheless, the complete revelation of God's fatherhood is only found in the record of the New Testament. Once the greater concept is established here, many of the fatherly features of God found in the Old Testament are enhanced in a most meaningful and personal way.

The Fatherhood of God as Revealed in the Four Gospels

I recently did a study of the four Gospels regarding all of the references to the fatherhood of God. Pertinent Scriptures were then categorized into the following four headings:

1. References that describe the unique family relationship between the Father and the Son which becomes a general model for us all.

   "We have beheld his glory, glory as of the only Son from the Father" (John 1:14, RSV).

2. References, usually by Jesus, that directly teach us about our own personal relationship as sons and daughters in the family of God.

   "If you then, who are evil, know how to give good gifts to your children, how much more will the heavenly Father give the Holy Spirit to those [of his children] who ask him!" (Luke 11:13, RSV).

3. Direct references to the fatherly characteristics of God based upon His attributes or behavior.

"Be merciful, even as your Father is merciful"
(Luke 6:36, RSV).

4. References to equality in nature between the
Father and the Son which allows the Son to
become a window through which the Father
may be known.

"Do you not believe that I am in the Father and
the Father in me? The words that I say to you I
do not speak on my own authority; but the
Father who dwells in me does his works" (John
14:10, RSV).

Obviously there is overlapping of the categories in some of
the passages, but the basic ideas are easily identified. An
interesting progression concerning the revelation of divine
fatherhood can clearly be traced throughout the Gospel
records.

Jesus: He Is the Son of God

In Luke's account of the geneology of Jesus Christ, he
traces His human ancestry all the way back to Adam, whom
he significantly describes as the son of God—an obvious
reference to God as the Father of the human race (Luke
3:38). This general concept, of course, as previously
discussed, was common knowledge among the Jewish
people. God was recognized as the Father-Creator of all
mankind. John's Gospel, however, begins by referring to
Jesus Christ as the pre-existent, co-existent, and divine
Word (Logos), which became flesh that the true glory of the
Father might be manifested to us. By receiving His Son, we
are given the right to become God's children.

One could paraphrase these portions found in that first
chapter of John as follows:

The Son existed in the beginning before all time. He was face-to-face with the Father, and together they expressed the timeless glory of God . . . But the Son took on the form of human flesh that the true and gracious nature of the Father might be expressed to those who had never seen Him. And, oh, the glory of it all, for they that received the Son were themselves given the wonderful privilege of becoming beloved children of God. (Adapted from John 1:1, 14, 18 and 12)

Now this concept of divine fatherhood was a new revelation to the everyday Jew on the street. John's record, of course, was written long after Jesus had lived, died, risen, and ascended to the Father. It will be of interest to trace how such an amazing revelation actually developed following the first advent of Jesus Christ to this world.

Again we must remember that although the prophets foresaw the coming of the Messiah, the average Jew did not appreciate the unique role He would play as the Son of God, because it involved a personal relationship with the Father which was foreign to his mentality and expectation.

The first reference to Christ's divine sonship in the synoptic Gospels is associated with Gabriel's visit to the virgin Mary concerning the birth of Jesus:

And, behold, thou shalt conceive in thy womb, and bring forth a son, and shalt call his name Jesus. He shall be great, and shall be called the Son of the Most High: . . . The Holy Ghost shall come upon thee, and the power of the Highest shall overshadow thee . . . therefore also that holy thing which shall be born of thee shall be called the Son of God. (Luke 1:31-32, 35)

Some months later a similar revelation is given to a bewildered Joseph in a dream. He is informed that Mary's child was conceived by the Holy Spirit, and that His name shall be called Emmanuel, which means, "God with us" (Matt. 1:20-24).

There were a few other indications to Mary and Joseph concerning the unique relationship which their son had with God:

1. Elizabeth saluted Mary as the "mother of my Lord" (Luke 1:43).
2. In the Magnificat, Mary's spirit rejoiced in "God, my Savior" (Luke 1:47).
3. The angel of the Lord identified the baby Jesus at His birth as the "Savior which is Christ the Lord" (Luke 2:11-12).
4. Simeon, at the presentation of Jesus in the temple, recognized Him as the "Lord's Christ" (Luke 2:26).
5. Joseph is warned in a dream to escape with Mary and Jesus to Egypt for their safety in fulfillment of the prophecy: "Out of Egypt did I call my son" (Matt. 2:15; Hos. 11:1).

Even these references, however, failed to reveal the intimate, personal communion which Jesus would later enjoy with His heavenly Father. Such a relationship with God was beyond their comprehension.

Nothing further is recorded concerning Christ's unique sonship with the Father until His twelfth year when Mary and Joseph were shocked to hear Jesus in the temple at Passover time explain to them that it was necessary for Him "to be in My Father's house and about My Father's business"

(Luke 2:49, TAB). Even then, the record reads, they were not able to comprehend what He was saying to them. Apparently His childhood must have demonstrated no miraculous or mysterious qualities which gave them reason to wonder about His special relationship to God.

The temple incident is very interesting, because it is the first time any reference is made concerning an awareness on the part of Jesus about His own personal relationship with the Father. How complete His understanding was, we do not know, but certainly He recognized the significance of His divine sonship at a level appropriate for His youthful age. There are some principles here which are worth pursuing.

Jesus truly is our elder and model Brother. We can look to His life for answers to questions which arise in our own if we are searching for understanding about divine fatherhood. He, too, had to make that discovery, because as a little baby, His concept of the heavenly Father was as limited as ours when we came into this world. How did Jesus, having assumed the limitations of our humanity, learn about the character of His heavenly Father?

Jesus Learns About the Fatherhood of God

As a little baby the first impressions of fatherhood obviously were learned from His relationship with Joseph. Some have perhaps unwittingly depreciated the role of Joseph in the life of Jesus because so little was entered into the record concerning their relationship. But God makes no mistakes, and the essential role of a father-figure for little Jesus was not left to chance. Joseph was chosen because he was a man of faith, obedience, loyalty, and above all, a man of humility and love. His character had been tested and proven before he was divinely directed to take Mary as his wife, and he was to little Jesus the earthly father-figure He would desperately need to fulfill His divine destiny as the

Son of Man. How wise and thoughtful of the heavenly Father to have chosen Joseph for such a special responsibility.

At a very early age baby Jesus learned to distinguish between the gentle loving arms of Mary, and the strong supporting arms of Joseph. There was the fragrance of freshly cut wood upon Joseph's clothes, mingled with the scent of honest sweat upon rough and calloused hands. Although a man of toil and hard labor, he always had time to take little Jesus along the back trails which crisscrossed the flower-spangled hills behind Nazareth. Perhaps it was from Joseph that Jesus learned about God's loving care for the little sparrows in the air, and the divine caress which graced the lovely lilies of the field.

As a small boy I am sure He was given minor tasks to perform in the carpenter shop where He loved to play with wooden blocks and leftover shavings. Undoubtedly it was here where He learned about a father's compassion and pity. Surely it was to Joseph's arms He ran when a minor mishap resulted in a cut finger. Joseph had a wise and loving way of comforting Jesus without leading Him into lingering attitudes of self-pity. Soon He was back at work or play, but a bit wiser for the experience.

Later as His responsibilities in the carpenter shop increased, Jesus learned how to select the proper woods and tools for various work projects. Possibly on some occasion Joseph sadly pointed out the kind of tree which was usually chosen for the making of the cruel Roman crosses. There may have followed some serious talk between a father and his son about the evil and injustice men inflict upon one another. How desperately the world needed a Messiah—someone who would heal the hurts of mankind and establish justice and righteousness in a world desperately sick with its own sin. Maybe this was something they talked about, and Jesus could see and feel the yearning and longing which filled the eyes and heart of Joseph.

Perhaps Jesus experienced the same feeling rising in His own heart when in the synagogue school He read and memorized the prophetic passages about a promised Messiah who, in spite of great suffering, would establish a kingdom of love and righteousness. How He must have earnestly prayed to God that the Messiah would hasten the day of His appearing.

Jesus learned the discipline and obedience necessary to master a trade. It was in the carpenter shop under Joseph's trained hand that He discovered the freedom and satisfaction of achievement that only the disciplined life can produce.

Still, there were disappointments, because He was also to learn the cruel, deceiving ways of man firsthand. How pleased Jesus had been with the first job He had completed all by himself. It felt so good to have the approval of Joseph, because he was a perfectionist in his work, and such praise was an indication of true achievement. How bewildered and hurt He had been when a prospective buyer had falsely belittled and downgraded His work in an endeavor to gain an unfair price advantage. It was Joseph, who with understanding, explained to Him the deceitful ways of worldly men.

Jesus had been deeply impressed by Joseph's remarks, because he had encouraged Him to measure everything in terms of God's standards rather than man's. Perhaps he had inspired Jesus to think of God as a true and loving Father whose gracious will should ever be our greatest desire to fulfill. The will of God was the most important goal on earth for which man should strive. Jesus had spent the rest of that night in prayer to God—His heavenly Father.

It was possibly for this reason that Jesus was so bewildered by His parents' concern for His whereabouts on that Passover trip to Jerusalem. Had not Joseph himself taught Him that the noblest purpose on earth was to be about "the Father's business"? It would appear that at twelve years of age the will of the Father was taking on deeper dimensions in His life than even Joseph could comprehend.

After the Death of Joseph

As the years passed, the boy Jesus grew in "wisdom and stature and in favor with God and man" (Luke 2:52). He became a competent carpenter, and following Joseph's death, assumed responsibility for Mary and the family. There was a time when I questioned what appeared to be an untimely death for Joseph. If I had been God, I would have had Joseph living to a ripe old age. He could have been Mary's companion after Jesus left home for His ministry, and obviously been her comfort and support throughout the ordeal of Christ's crucifixion. Both Mary and Joseph could have been with the disciples on the day of Pentecost, and experienced the joy of establishing the church which their Son had founded.

However, God does all things well and always in harmony with His holy will. I have since come to believe there was divine purpose in Joseph's death which can be of great comfort for those who have committed their lives to God's will here on earth. Joseph had a special call and commission from God for his place and time in the divine plan. Through Joseph's life little Jesus learned about the fatherhood of God. There came a time in the young manhood of Jesus when His dependency upon Joseph as a father-figure was totally transferred to His heavenly Father. A communion with God was established which no longer required the intermediary of an earthly father. Jesus knew who He was, and the unique relationship which was divinely His as God's Son.

Joseph had fulfilled his role well; nothing was left undone or unfinished. It was as if God looking down with great satisfaction, lovingly called Joseph home, for his divine task was now complete. I am sure Jesus, himself, comforted Mary in the loss of a good and faithful husband with the assurance that his earthly work had come to an end, and God's great redemptive plan would soon be fulfilled. As always, Mary held such mysteries in her heart, and lovingly and obediently submitted to the will of God.

An elderly friend of ours who has had a proven ministry over many years once shared with me a vision she had of Jesus prior to His earthly ministry. He had just completed construction of a table-like bench, and was brushing away the remaining traces of sawdust with the sensitive touch of a master craftsman. He was lean and muscular in physique, and she particularly noticed the callouses on His hands. She realized there was something special about the occasion, and was impressed in her spirit that this was the last piece of work that He would ever accomplish in the carpentry shop. She was caused to know that He worked very hard during the day, but spent many hours in the night communing with His heavenly Father.

He carefully placed His tools in their designated places, folded His apron, and laid it upon a bench. He then moved directly to the door, turning only once to survey the familiar surroundings of the workshop He had inherited from Joseph following his death. He had followed in the footsteps of Joseph for many years, but the time had now come to minister the words and works of His heavenly Father, and fulfill His divine calling. After His brief pause—so much can be gathered up during such moments—He decisively shut the door . . . And my friend knew deep in her spirit that He was on His way to the Jordan to meet John.

Behold the Lamb of God

It had been almost eighteen years since Jesus confessed His need and desire to be about His Father's business. A new aspect of this divine relationship with God is about to be emphasized—a revelation from the Father himself.

Jesus, as God's sinless Son, submitted himself to John's baptism of repentance, thereby identifying himself with sinful humanity. It was also an act of loving obedience to His heavenly Father who had sent His only Son into this world to restore a loving family relationship which had long since been destroyed by man's rebellion.

There is a heavenly beauty to this unique baptismal scene, because God's redeeming love was being brought into full view in the person of God's only Son.

For thirty years the Father has waited for this occasion, then He speaks and Jesus, the carpenter's son, is publicly recognized as the Son of God:

This is my beloved Son, in whom I am well pleased. (Matt. 3:17)

John, witnessing the descent of the Holy Spirit upon Jesus, later declared:

And I have seen and have borne witness that this is the Son of God. (John 1:34, RSV)

The next day John, upon seeing Jesus again, informs two of his disciples (Andrew and John) that He is indeed the Lamb of God. They immediately follow Him, and are later joined by Peter, Philip, and Nathanael. Nathanael is so impressed he spontaneously exclaims, "Rabbi, you are the Son of God! You are the King of Israel!" (John 1:49, RSV). This may have been a reference to one of the prophetic passages in the Old Testament:

> Yet have I set my king upon my holy hill of Zion. I
> will declare the decree: the Lord hath said unto me,
> Thou art my Son; this day have I begotten thee.
> (Ps. 2:6-7)

Nathanael's perception of Jesus along with the other disciples, while rudimentary and simplistic, was nevertheless very real and personal. It would take time for the true significance of Christ's sonship to develop, but for the most part, this would gradually come by way of Christ's own words and teaching.

Sonship, of course, involves the companion concept of fatherhood; it is the other side of the coin. It is not surprising, therefore, in tracing the early ministry of Jesus, that many references were made by the Lord to His heavenly Father. Surely, after hearing Jesus pray, the disciples must have discussed among themselves how He indeed viewed God in a most intimate way as His very own Father. This personal dimension of divine fatherhood was a new idea for them, but most assuredly one which held great fascination. It was, in fact, their preparation for realizing their own personal relationship with God as their heavenly Father.

Your Father in Heaven

It was one thing to think of Jesus as experiencing a loving, caring relationship with His heavenly Father, but quite another to imagine that something this divine could include a whole family of sons and daughters. Surely the disciples had no idea that they were soon to be introduced to a concept of personal sonship by which they, too, could think of God as a holy, but compassionate Father.

The time which Jesus chose for this remarkable revelation was associated with one of the most important and decisive occasions of His early ministry. So significant was the event, that Jesus had spent the entire night in prayer with His heavenly Father. In the morning He chose twelve apostles from His many followers. It would be their privilege to be intimately associated with Him for special teaching and training. God's eternal purpose for the Church and His kingdom for a time would primarily rest upon their shoulders. How very little they could foresee of the unexpected events which would follow their commitment to Christ.

One wonders how Jesus might introduce the disciples to the character of His kingdom, and the principles upon which it would be based. Perhaps they wondered, too. Their curiosity was short-lived, however, because Jesus immediately brought them together apart from, but in the presence of, a great multitude.

The Sermon on the Mount was their inaugural address. They listened in amazement as Jesus clearly cut through the outward forms and earthly interpretations of Jewish law, and uncovered the heavenly purpose and power for which and by which it could be fulfilled. They were astounded to discover that God's holy will could only be accomplished here on earth as they would cease from their own efforts and totally rely upon an inner relationship with God as their heavenly Father.

So often we have emphasized the kingdom theme of the Sermon on the Mount that we have failed to see that the government of God rests squarely upon a royal family relationship with the Father. What holy wonder must have filled their hearts as again and again they heard Jesus describe their relationship with God in the same terms with which He described His own. This was their introduction to

God as beloved sons whose life relationship with the heavenly Father was something to be felt with their hearts.

Put yourself in their place, and listen with your heart to the words of Jesus concerning the Father-heart of God as we have listed them from Christ's sermon on that special and wonderful day:

> Blessed are the peacemakers, for they shall be called sons of God. (Matt. 5:9, RSV)
> Let your light so shine before men, that they may see your good works and give glory to your Father who is in heaven. (Matt. 5:16, RSV)
> But I say to you, Love your enemies and pray for those who persecute you, so that you may be sons of your Father who is in heaven. (Matt. 5:44-45, RSV)
> You, therefore, must be perfect, as your heavenly Father is perfect. (Matt. 5:48, RSV)
> But love your enemies. . . and your reward will be great, and you will be sons of the Most High; for he is kind to the ungrateful and the selfish. Be merciful, even as your Father is merciful. (Luke 6:35-36, RSV)
> Beware of practicing your piety before men in order to be seen by them; for then you will have no reward from your Father who is in heaven. (Matt. 6:1, RSV)
> [May your alms] be in secret; and your Father who sees in secret will reward you. (Matt. 6:4, RSV)
> But when you pray, go into your room and shut the door and pray to your Father who is in secret; and your Father who sees in secret will reward you. (Matt. 6:6, RSV)
> Do not be like them [repetitious Gentiles], for

your Father knows what you need before you ask him. Pray then like this: Our Father, who art in heaven, hallowed be thy name. (Matt. 6:8-9, RSV)
For if you forgive men their trespasses, your heavenly Father also will forgive you; but if you do not forgive men their trespasses, neither will your Father forgive your trespasses. (Matt. 6:14-15, RSV)
[Fast not to] be seen by men but by your Father who is in secret; and your Father who sees in secret will reward you. (Matt. 6:18, RSV)
Look at the birds of the air: they neither sow nor reap nor gather into barns, and yet your heavenly Father feeds them. (Matt. 6:26, RSV)
Therefore do not be anxious, saying, "What shall we eat . . . drink . . . wear?" Your heavenly Father knows that you need them all. (Matt. 6:31-32, RSV)
If you then, who are evil, know how to give good gifts to your children, how much more will your Father who is in heaven give good things to those who ask him! (Matt. 7:11, RSV)

No wonder Matthew observed that the crowds were astonished at Christ's teachings. A new concept of kingdom living had been presented within the context of a royal family of which God was the heavenly Father. Jesus had spoken with recognized authority, and little wonder, because they were the words of God's very own Son!

The Sermon on the Mount contains more direct references to God as our heavenly Father than any other teaching in the Gospels. Even the farewell discourse by Jesus in John's Gospel (chapters 14-17), which greatly extends our understanding of divine fatherhood, almost exclusively uses the phrases, "My Father" or "The Father." However, because of the personal relationship previously established in the Sermon on the Mount, we can very warmly respond to any reference in Scripture which includes the theme of divine fatherhood.

The Character of Our Heavenly Father

Once the fatherhood of God and our sonship and daughterhood are established, the wonderful nature of that relationship is enhanced as we become better acquainted with what the Father is really like. We made brief reference to this important theme in our first chapter when we considered some of the functions which divine fatherhood fulfills. We can find many references to our Father's loving provision, protection, direction, correction, and redeeming grace throughout the Scriptures. The shepherd-heart of our heavenly Father desires that not one of His little lambs be lost, but that all should be brought into the fold of His love. The waywardness of a stubborn sheep brings pain to both the sheep and the shepherd, but mercy reaches out to the farthest mountainside to reclaim the wounded wanderer (Matt. 18:10-14). The wages of sin reveal the folly of the self-willed life, and were divinely designed to open our hearts to the redemptive power of God's grace, and the wisdom of His will for our lives (Jer. 2:19). Sadly, some must face death before they are ready to receive the Father's gift of eternal life (Rom. 6:23).

If we were to choose one passage that might best portray to us this loving heart of God, perhaps it would be the parable of the prodigal son. Actually this story of God's love as told by Jesus might far better have been titled, "The Parable of the Forgiving Father," because there we find a perfect portrait of our Father God (Luke 15:11-32). Usually this story is told from the perspective of the wayward son, but rich insight can be gained by keeping the focus upon the character of the father himself.

He had lovingly raised two sons who were heirs of his entire household and estate. They both had futures bright with personal promise and fulfillment because of their father's provision. Under his hand they had been trained to wisely administer their inheritance. All the privileges and responsibilities of true sonship were theirs. It was only a matter of time when they would be raising their own families, as an extended expression of their father's faithfulness. In every possible way the father had shared both his life and love with his two dear sons.

Outwardly everything appeared to be in order, but inwardly both sons suffered from a sickness of heart. Neither was serving his father from an inner attitude of love and appreciation. The privilege of their father's presence and loving purpose was taken for granted, and for the younger son even became a source of irritation. Father's house for him was more of a prison than a place of promise.

He requested and received, as was his legal right, his portion of the inheritance, and immediately set out to experience the freedom and fulfillment which he felt could only be achieved in a far and foreign country. It is of interest to note that his father did not resist his son's decision, nor did he send an entourage of servants for his care and protection. The father respected the sovereignty of his son's life and did not interfere even though he knew what the ultimate outcome of such a choice would be. His father-heart was saddened by his son's rebellion, and he grieved over the inevitable affliction his son was soon to suffer as a result of his own willful way, but he let him go.

The wayward son enjoyed the pleasures of sin for a season, but eventually his father's bounty was depleted. A famine spread across the land, and the son soon discovered the loneliness and loss which are inevitable results of "far-country" living. Fancy friends, food, and pleasures were ironically replaced by pigs, husks, and humiliation. Then the record reads, "He came to himself."

Throughout the entire time of the son's absence his father did not personally seek him for either revenge or rescue. He prayerfully waited while his son reaped the full harvest of his own willful way. (Sometimes we blame the Lord for the grievous consequences of our own rebellion. God's discipline for our lives, however, usually is in the harvest we reap from the seeds of our own disobedience.)

It was at this point that the wayward son made a marvelous discovery: While it is possible to leave father's house, it is impossible to get beyond the reach of father's love. What had been set within his life in father's house now brought hope to his heart as he headed homeward trusting solely in his father's lovingkindness and tender mercy. Nor was he disappointed, because "while he was yet at a distance, his father saw him and had great compassion, and ran and embraced him and kissed him." The ring, robe, shoes, and feast were in sharp contrast to his recent experience in the pigpen. The younger son had not only come to himself, he had at last really discovered his true identity—in his father's house.

Not so for the elder son. Ever since the departure of his younger brother—an independence he may have secretly envied—his service for his father had become a grim duty, completely disassociated from the privilege of his position as a beloved elder son. Jealousy and bitterness filled his soul. In one sense he had been as far from his father's home and heart as had his younger brother. Purposely Jesus left the ultimate outcome of the elder son's attitude unsaid for it was a perfect picture of the Pharisee of that day. What an unlovely description of those who are devoid of grace and forgiveness. Sadly, it is also a portrait of the Pharisees of every age. No wonder the concept of a forgiving Father-God has been so distorted in the minds of many who desperately need to be assured of His tender mercy. How wise and wonderful it was of Jesus to include in His ministry this parable about the true nature of our dear heavenly Father.

Jesus made many other references to the loving-caring character of the Father in the many Scripture references already listed. But, besides the understanding gained through His sermons, the greatest demonstration of the Father's nature was personally expressed by His very life.

I and the Father Are One

Of all of the disciples, perhaps Philip was the most pragmatic. His little computer-like brain could always come up with a mental readout based on things as they naturally appeared. Prior to the miraculous feeding of the five thousand, it was Philip who quickly calculated the dollars-and-cents cost-per-serving, and promptly advised the Lord there was no way such a crowd could be fed. It was difficult for him to break beyond the earthly scene into the limitless realm of the Spirit (John 6:1-13).

We are not too surprised, therefore, that during the upper room discourse (John 14) Philip interrupts the Lord with another of his practical suggestions. Jesus had been assuring them that He himself would be their guarantee of a place in the Father's house. Every member in the household of God has a special place and purpose in the eternal plan of the divine Godhead. Such a celestial concept of the Father's purpose for a royal family was far beyond Philip's earthly mentality. He strains to reduce the reality of the Father's divine plan to a physical picture which they could behold with their eyes. If the Lord would only show them the Father, their puzzled and perplexed minds would be satisfied.

I am sure the expression on the face of Jesus must have

40

shown His deep disappointment. His response rises from His heart, and perhaps might be expressed in the following expanded paraphrase:

> Philip, oh, Philip, have I been with you so long, and you say show us the Father? Have I not said that I and my Father are one, and that He is in me, and I in Him? (John 10:30, 38). The words which I speak are not my words, but His; the works which I do are not my works, but those of my Father. Philip, don't you understand; if you have seen me, you have seen Him. When you look upon my face, it is His features which you behold. The warmth which you feel in your heart and the enlightenment which comes to your mind when I speak is because I only proclaim His words of love and truth. When you are close enough to embrace me, you have embraced Him. Philip, when you reached me, you reached the Father!
> I am the only way you can truly know what the Father's life is really like. I am that life, and as you abide in me and I in you, that life can be personally yours as well. The reality of the Father is not something you picture in your mind, Philip, but something that is experienced in your life. After I return to the Father, you shall through His Spirit come to really know Him more truly than an earthly son knows his own father.

I am sure the disciples tried to grasp the meaning of Christ's words, but the full significance of that revelation was to await the coming of the Comforter who, as the Spirit of Truth, would bring all things to their remembrance and quicken their understanding.

That the Holy Spirit was faithful in that ministry is proven years later by the opening words of both John's Gospel and his first epistle. With profound understanding he proclaims that Jesus Christ was indeed the Living Word. The Word about the life and love of the Father had truly become flesh—hearable, seeable, touchable—in the person of His own Son.

> That which was from the beginning, which we have heard, which we have seen with our eyes, which we have looked upon and touched with our hands, concerning the word of life—the life was made manifest, and we saw it, and testify to it, and proclaim to you the eternal life which was with the Father and was made manifest to us—that which we have seen and heard we proclaim also to you, so that you may have fellowship with us; and our fellowship is with the Father and with his Son Jesus Christ. (1 John 1:1-3, RSV)

This concept of knowing the Father through the Son becomes a key to discovering a new dimension in the records of Christ's earthly life.

Suffer the Little Children to Come unto Me

Christ is indeed the key which reveals to us the true character of our heavenly Father. This means His whole life as recorded in the Gospels was like a picture of the Father being painted by the brush strokes of divine words and deeds. What added insight this truth brings to our study of the Gospels. One particular incident illustrates this point in a very beautiful and wonderful way. The story is recorded for us in the tenth chapter of Mark's Gospel.

Jesus had spent considerable time discussing the matter

of marriage and divorce with the Pharisees, who purposely had come to engage Him in dispute and argumentation. Later the Lord and His disciples retreated indoors perhaps to the home of a guest. The disciples raised further questions concerning some of the difficult aspects of such marital matters. Jesus was probably very tired, but graciously and patiently responded to the troublesome items which still plagued their minds.

At this point the Scriptures say that some little children were brought to Him, probably by their parents. Possibly they were trying to gain entrance to the house, or as one commentator suggests, they may have been the children of the household who were introduced to Jesus for His blessing before going to bed. That indeed would be a tender touch to the story.

Obviously the parents sensed something of God's love in Jesus, and wanted their little children to be blessed and caressed by the Lord. They must have approached Jesus with a sense of warm expectation. I have tried to imagine the expression on the bright little faces of the children, as they looked up into the beautiful, loving eyes of Jesus. (I have always pictured Jesus with crinkle-marks by His eyes.) Such a lovely scene hardly prepares us for the rude response which follows.

The disciples, perhaps partly to protect their tired teacher, but maybe to relieve their own annoyance by such an interruption, sternly rebuke the parents and roughly push the children away from the Lord. There is a sudden change in attitude on the part of Jesus as with great indignation He turns to the disciples and sharply informs them that little children and the kingdom of God belong very much together.

Once again His eyes soften and with outstretched arms He reassures the parents and calls the little ones unto himself.

The Scriptures state that He took them in His arms one by one and placed His hands upon them, and fervently blessed them (Mark 10:16, TAB). I am so glad Jesus didn't suggest they group all the children together for a sort of general blessing because He was rather tired. Instead, He took time to hold each child close to His heart and to earnestly pray for them all . . . they then joyfully scampered off to bed.

One is tenderly reminded of a beautiful messianic passage from the prophets:

> He will feed His flock like a shepherd, He will gather the lambs in His arm, He will carry them in His bosom, and will gently lead those that have their young. (Isa. 40:11, TAB)

Besides the deeper truths concerning the character of the kingdom, what else is Jesus trying to convey through this vivid account recorded in all three of the synoptic Gospels? Isn't this a perfect picture of the lovingkindness of our heavenly Father? It is as if Jesus is saying, "Look, this is the way your Father-God feels about you. He wants to hug you to His heart, and personally bless your life with His love and mercy." I think there is also a lesson here for any who would seek to set any kind of false condition concerning just who should be recipients of God's grace. He blessed them all!

We have discovered what a beautiful portrait of our heavenly Father is presented to us through a study of the Gospels. An even greater appreciation of our Father-God will arise in our hearts and minds as we move to the New Testament portions which involve the early Church after Pentecost. Here we shall discover that both the person and purpose of the Father are wonderfully wedded together. And marvel of marvels, we all play an important part in His gracious and glorious plan!

3

The Fatherhood of God in the Early Church

Words are fascinating structures of speech. Linked together they form the line of communication which joins our hearts and minds. They are the means by which what is on the inside of you can get on the inside of me. Words not only convey meaning, they have both creative and destructive power and can exert an important influence on how we think, feel, and subsequently behave.

Words also have characteristics which sometimes are related in description to the perceptions of our physical senses. For instance:

Some words are warm, others cool.
Some words are soft, others hard.
Some words are smooth, others rough.
Some words are sweet, others bitter.
Some words are fragrant, others foul.
Some words heal, others hurt.

Many words even have color. The word anger is associated with the color red. The word melancholy actually means black bile. Sometimes when we are sad we say we are feeling blue.

For most people the word truth is associated with whiteness. Often it is a very sterile, almost hospital-like white, with faint traces of ether or antiseptic! On the other hand the word love usually brings to mind some of the soft, warm pastel colors such as floral pinks and yellows. Such colors have corresponding feelings with obvious subconscious undertones. (Now we can better appreciate the necessity of always linking love and truth together. The soft warmth of love enables us to receive the bright sterilizing power of the truth.)

Subconscious Attitudes About the Father

As the reader may have already surmised, the above observations have been made during various meetings where people were given the opportunity to respond with the different color-word combinations. Such word association exercises often reveal some of our inner emotions which have been buried below our level of conscious thought.

For instance, what color comes to your mind when we say the word judge? The usual response is black, and we visualize someone behind a high bench in black robes. Now let's try another word and you respond with the first color that comes to your mind. The word is father.

If fatherhood is associated with a loving personal relationship, perhaps some of the warmer, softer colors came to mind. For some, however, the word father and judge are almost synonymous, and subconsciously associated with the color black. Maybe the black robe has a sterile white collar to go with it, if we are apprehensively thinking of justice without mercy.

For many, some of the same feelings may carry over to their concept of a holy Father-God. They picture Him more as a judge with a frown on his face than as a loving Father who views them in a kindly fashion.

A Fearful Father Image

Another question which can reveal something of our subconscious attitude toward God concerns our feelings when we have failed and desperately need His forgiveness. In our minds, is it easier to go to our holy, heavenly Father, or our Redeemer-brother Jesus with our confession? Most people readily admit they feel less apprehensive in taking their fault to the Lord Jesus.

Now it is true, Christ is our mediator, and the only way to the Father in a theological sense, but the above concern relates more to a subconscious feeling that Jesus might be a little more sympathetic. In fact, for some we picture the Lord as endeavoring to persuade the Father to withhold His wrath and great indignation. It is as if the Father has to be pacified before He will express a more lenient attitude toward our faults and failures. We are not talking here about the necessity of the atonement wherein Christ's death satisfied the demands of the law, but basic feelings concerning the personalities in the Godhead. To put the issue more directly, many subconsciously feel that the Son has a more forgiving nature than the Father, though they probably would hesitate to put their subsurface sentiment that directly.

Such a fearful attitude, when deeply rooted in our lives, leaves us with continual feelings of guilt and condemnation. Therefore, it is difficult to believe that we are fully accepted and approved by our heavenly Father—much less to consider ourselves as a source of His joy and pleasure. We cannot help seeing a stern judge on his throne, rather than a loving Father in our heavenly home!

While many do not suffer from such a severe picture as we

have painted, some do, and others have honestly confessed that they have a tendency at times to harbor similar feelings. These observations have been repeatedly confirmed in meetings with Christians of diverse denominational backgrounds.

Where and when did such a mentality concerning the severity of the Father begin? Jesus certainly didn't present the Father in this light, as we have already seen. Did the leaders in the early New Testament church contribute to such a concept? What was the thinking and feeling of the writers of the epistles concerning the fatherhood of God? Let us return to the Scriptures again and see what we can find that will help us to understand the problem. Certainly something this significant to so many individuals demands an answer. For many it could lead to a whole new relationship with their heavenly Father.

The Father in Christ's Farewell Address and Intercessory Prayer

Just before His crucifixion, Christ gathered the disciples to encourage and prepare them for the immediate crisis, and then to fix their faith for the future (John 14-17). The events of the next two months would set the hinge of history upon which the divine door of redemptive purpose would swing open for all eternity. The disciples were soon to experience the full forces of both hell and heaven as they entered into the reality of the crucifixion, resurrection, ascension, and Pentecost.

I am sure they sensed in their spirits the urgency and importance of that pivotal hour in history, but could not comprehend with their understanding the full magnitude of all that was soon to transpire. No wonder they were perplexed in mind and disturbed at heart as Jesus began to reveal to them both the tragedy and glory of those decisive days just before them.

With great compassion and understanding Jesus promises them that they will not be left alone as orphans, but the Father himself would provide another Comforter who would instruct and empower their lives for a ministry which in works and witness would exceed even His own. What a staggering statement that must have been to men who had never dreamed that Jesus might someday leave them. Their concept of the kingdom had always centered around Christ as an earthly king whose personal presence was the key to their whole future.

Then Jesus seeks to assure them that the fulfillment of divine purpose rests upon an intimate relationship which they will have—through the Holy Spirit—with the Father. He emphatically informs them four times over that they are personally loved by the Father. Indeed, the Father loves them as He loves the Son! (John 14:21, 23; 16:27; 17:23).

On the basis of this love relationship they now can do something they never yet have done—they can pray directly to the Father in Christ's name, and He will answer their prayers as readily as He answered the prayers of Jesus (John 16:23-27). In other words, Christ is preparing the disciples for their apostolic ministry following His ascension. They were to have an intimate, personal relationship with the Father based on His love.

The Holy Spirit is often referred to as the "Spirit of Christ" which would indwell and empower their lives after Pentecost. I think it is interesting, however, that Jesus himself once referred to the Holy Spirit as the "Spirit of the Father" (Matt. 10:20). The Holy Spirit provides the basis for an abiding relationship in God. Jesus referred to His abiding in the Father, and the Father abiding in Him (John 14:11). We are to abide in Christ, and He in us (John 15:4). But there is also an intimate abiding relationship with the Father, for

His beloved sons and daughters:

> In that day you will know that I am in my Father,
> and you in me, and I in you. (John 14:20, RSV)
> If a man loves me, he will keep my word, and my
> Father will love him, and we will come to him, and
> make our home [abode] with him. (John 14:23, RSV)
> I do not pray for these only, but also for those who
> believe in me through their word, that they may all
> be one; even as thou, Father, art in me, and I in
> thee, that they also may be in us, so that the world
> may believe that thou hast sent me. (John 17:20-21,
> RSV)

Obviously, Jesus was leading the disciples (and us) into an understanding of true spiritual sonship and daughterhood. It is as if Jesus was saying, "The same relationship I enjoy with the Father is to be yours as well. From this will come your authority and power as members of God's royal family." The disciples were repeatedly reminded of the reality of that relationship throughout the entire farewell discourse and prayer when Jesus used the word Father over fifty times.

The Apostolic Concept of Fatherhood

We must turn to the epistles to discover the attitude of the apostles after Pentecost to the fatherhood of God. Did the revelation to the disciples of their new relationship with the Father through the Holy Spirit develop as intended for their lives? What can we discover from the tone and content of their writings about their personal attitude and relationship to God the Father?

Of the original twelve disciples, perhaps John, in his first epistle, most warmly and personally portrays the new family relationship with God, which is the true basis for both earthly and heavenly fellowship. John's primary purpose in writing the epistle was to counteract some fundamental errors, particularly gnosticism, which was creeping into the early church. The latter teaching denied the incarnation of Christ, and in his defense of Christ's divine sonship, John beautifully describes the Father-family relationship which is the privilege of every believer. The first two verses of his second chapter most concisely confirm this personal concept of divine fatherhood:

> See how very much our heavenly Father loves us, for he allows us to be called his children—think of it—and we really are! But since most people don't know God, naturally they don't understand that we are his children. Yes, dear friends, we are already God's children, right now, and we can't even imagine what it is going to be like later on. But we do know this, that when he comes we will be like him, as a result of seeing him as he really is. And everyone who really believes this will try to stay pure because Christ is pure. (1 John 3:1-3, TLB)

Another of the foremost writers in the early years of the Church was the Apostle Paul. His conversion on the Damascus Road came after the Church was already founded (Acts 9), and we might have reason to question his understanding of divine fatherhood, since he was not among the original disciples. Paul does not leave us in doubt, however, for he carefully explains that his gospel came as a direct revelation from Christ himself. Furthermore, he recognized that he had been chosen by the Father before he was born, and was given a revelation of the divine purpose in Christ Jesus for the entire Gentile world (Gal. 1:11-12,

15-16).

Again, in another epistle he refers to a precise, personal experience where he had been caught up into the third heaven (presence of God) where he heard "sacred secrets" beyond the limitations of earthly speech (2 Cor. 12:1-4). Perhaps included in this divine revelation were the mysteries concerning the nature and purpose for the great family of God which the apostle refers to in his other epistles. Certainly in Paul we have an anointed authority concerning the fatherhood of God. We shall want to carefully explore what further insights we may gain from his writings.

One interesting observation can be made immediately: All of Paul's epistles begin with a salutation recognizing the heavenly Father. Here is a typical greeting:

> Paul, an apostle of Christ Jesus by the will of God, and Timothy our brother. To the church of God which is at Corinth . . . Grace to you and peace from God our Father and the Lord Jesus Christ. Blessed be the God and Father of our Lord Jesus Christ, the Father of mercies and God of all comfort. (2 Cor. 1:1-3, RSV)

One readily feels a warm sense of affection and personal appreciation for the fatherliness of God.

It is, however, in the content of Paul's epistles that the person and purpose of the heavenly Father is developed with a depth which obviously is born from the lofty perspective of heavenly revelation. Paul pushes past the boundaries of time and touches the eternal heart-desire of the Father himself. It centers in a love relationship with the Son as they are selflessly united in the beautiful but mystical communion of the Holy Spirit. The great Father-heart of God longs for the lovely life of His delightful Son to be extended in a family of many sons and daughters who would each uniquely express that life as they were so created.

For this reason was man fashioned from this earth, and given authority over every living thing. To him alone was given the command to be fruitful and fill the whole earth and subdue it. This was God's plan for the expansion of a royal family that would become His universal joy and delight. Sadly, the very first family rebelled and sought to fulfill their lives apart from God's will, thereby separating the human family from the Father's ultimate purpose. God was not caught off guard, however, for redemptive purpose had been a foreseen part of the original creation. That purpose was achieved through God's Son—our Redeemer-brother—for the divine plan was destined to succeed.

Through Christ Jesus we still have a royal destiny, for wonder of wonders, the Father has willed us to be joint-heirs with His Son as we move into the coming kingdom-age. As Paul expressed it, words fail to convey the magnitude and magnificence of God's amazing plan for His beloved sons and daughters. We are overwhelmed!

A Key That Enhances Our Concept of Divine Fatherhood in the Epistles

In tracing the theme of fatherhood through the Pauline epistles, I made an interesting discovery which greatly enhanced my understanding. We shall mention it here for it adds a dimension to some of Paul's writings which we shall subsequently wish to consider in greater depth. In fact it is a key which works in all of the New Testament Scriptures.

Many times when the word God or Lord is used, it is obvious from the context that the reference is to God the Father, or at least the emphasis is on the first member of the Trinity. For example, one of the most familiar passages in Scripture reads as follows:

> For God so loved the world, that he gave his only
> begotten Son, that whosoever believeth in him
> should not perish but have everlasting life. (John
> 3:16)

We could, therefore, rephrase this passage in a more
personal way without changing the basic message:

> For our own dear heavenly Father so loved each
> one of us that He gave His only Son, that by
> believing in Him we might not lose our place in His
> beloved family, but joyfully live together forever.

By substituting a phrase such as "our dear heavenly
Father" for the word "God" where appropriate, our personal
appreciation of the Father's loving nature is greatly
enhanced.

Consider some similar paraphrases from Paul's writings
as so modified from the Living Bible:

> Long ago, even before he made the world, [our
> dear heavenly Father] chose us to be his very own,
> through what Christ would do for us; [our Father]
> decided then to make us holy in his eyes, without a
> single fault—we who stand before him covered
> with his love. [Father's] unchanging plan has
> always been to adopt us into his own family by
> sending Jesus Christ to die for us. And [our loving
> heavenly Father] did this because he wanted to!
> (Eph. 1:4-5)
> For from the very beginning [our dear Father] God
> decided that those who came to him—and all along
> he knew who would—should become like his Son,

so that his Son would be the First, with many brothers. And having chosen us, [our Father] called us to come to him; and when we came, [Father] declared us "not guilty," filled us with Christ's goodness, gave us right standing with himself, and promised us his glory. What can we ever say to such wonderful things as these? If [our blessed heavenly Father] is on our side, who can ever be against us? (Rom. 8:29-31)

Obviously there are many more such passages scattered throughout Paul's writings. Perhaps the reader may wish to make this a study for himself. I would recommend starting with the book of Ephesians.

Something is happening to our concept of fatherhood as we have developed our study thus far. We find nothing that implies that somehow the Father has to be persuaded to express His love and forgiveness towards us. In fact, we gain the feeling it was His loving plan all along to bring us back into His good graces.

Perhaps the following passage will bring into a fixed and final focus all that we have been trying to say about the loving nature of our Father-God. Again from one of Paul's letters we read these amazing words:

All these new things are from [our dear heavenly Father], who brought us back to himself through what Christ Jesus did. And [our Father] has given us the privilege of urging everyone to come into his favor and be reconciled to him. For God [our own dear Father] was in Christ, restoring the world to himself, no longer counting men's sins against them but blotting them out. This is the wonderful message [our Father] has given us to tell others. (2 Cor. 5:18-20, TLB)

What a different picture of God this brings to our hearts and minds. The redemption of sinful man was actually something the Father and Son had planned together before the foundation of the world.

Abraham A Type of Divine Fatherhood

One is reminded of the story of Abraham and Isaac when the former's love for God was put to the ultimate test. Would he be willing to sacrifice Isaac, his only and beloved son, on the mountain of Moriah? Isaac, of course, is a type of Christ. It was upon his back the sacrificial wood was carried, and as the Scripture twice records, "they went both of them together" (Gen. 22:1-14). We are told that Abraham bound Isaac and laid him on the altar. Now Isaac was in his late teens or early twenties, and could easily have overcome his elderly father if he had not chosen to submit in obedience. Perhaps he had pled with his father, Abraham, if there wasn't some other way God's demand could be met. When assured there was no other way, Isaac became a willing sacrifice. Possibly he entered into the faith of his father, that God could raise him from the dead, and thereby fulfill his destiny as the son of promise (Heb. 11:17-18). As Abraham raises the knife you recall, he was stopped by the angel of the Lord and informed of a substitutionary ram caught in a nearby thicket. Abraham's faith had been more than matched by God's grace!

Sometimes we fail to appreciate that Abraham was also a type of our heavenly Father. It must have been an agonizing journey for Abraham as he sought to prove his love and faith in God. Even the hope of a resurrection could not have dulled the pain that would be in a father's heart on such an occasion. Perhaps this is a small picture of the agony and pain our heavenly Father experienced when His own beloved Son was not spared the anguish of the cross.

Abba, Father!

We also are reminded of the heart-cry of God's own Son as He approached His Mount Moriah in the Garden of Gethsemane:

> Abba, Father, all things are possible to thee; remove this cup from me; yet not what I will, but what thou wilt. (Mark 14:36, RSV)

The phrase "Abba, Father" is most meaningful on this occasion for it contains an intimate insight into the Father-family relationship. It is used only three times in Scripture. The other two passages relate to our divine sonship and daughterhood:

> For you did not receive the spirit of slavery to fall back into fear, but you have received the spirit of sonship. When we cry, "Abba! Father!" it is the Spirit himself bearing witness with our spirit that we are children of God. (Rom. 8:15-16, RSV)
> And because you are sons, God has sent the Spirit of his Son into our hearts, crying, "Abba! Father!" (Gal. 4:6, RSV)

Abba is an Aramaic term of personal endearment akin to our "papa" or "daddy." It is the affectionate language of a child who looks to his father for faithful provision and protection. It is a term of trust which is based upon a personal love relationship.

The term father implies a more mature relationship of a respectful son who is ready to obediently assume both authority and responsibility in the family. It is a term of trust based upon the proven faithfulness of the father. Experience has established the truth that Father always keeps His word. We might outline these thoughts below before commenting further:

Abba	**Father**
1. Papa—daddy	Sir
2. Unreasoned affection	Reasoned respect
3. Love—trust	Truth—trust
4. Provision—protection	Authority—responsibility
5. Simplicity	Maturity
6. Childhood	Sonship—daughterhood

The *Abba* relationship of childhood is never lost even after we have matured into full sonship and daughterhood with the "Father." Particularly in times of crisis, demand, or serious decision, little boy and little girl feelings may momentarily rush to the surface of our hearts. Such feelings of dependency on our heavenly Father are not wrong, but actually provide the basis upon which mature behavior can confidently rest. Actually, we are on dangerous ground if we ever move away from our childlike dependency upon God. The full power and authority of the kingdom is determined by daily confessing as little children the faithfulness of our heavenly Father. Then we are ready to move on through the gates to the full responsibility of kingdom-living as royal sons and daughters.

It is rather comforting to know that Jesus, in His humanity, in His greatest hour of crisis, cried out to His *Abba* for comfort, reassurance, and love. Yet this was without weakness or compromise, because immediately the full responsibility of sonship was expressed as Christ emphatically confessed that the will of His heavenly Father would be done.

The relationship of love, faith, and obedience between the Son and His Father found their finest expression in that hour of divine decision. The Son turned to His Father in this time of terrifying anticipation and accepted the assurance of His presence. He then resolutely submitted to His will, confident that the Father's love would ultimately triumph over sin, Satan, hell, and the grave. "Abba, Father" took on its full meaning—the confession of an earthly Son to His heavenly Father from a heart filled with faith, hope, and love!

Broken Fellowship with the Father: A Double Tragedy

We should emphasize at this point that it wasn't the physical pain of Christ's forthcoming crucifixion which caused His soul to recoil in horror; it was the reality that He, the pure, holy, sinless Son of God, was about to become sin and in His humanity suffer its consequences—broken fellowship with the Father. Soon He would actually experience the awful loneliness and terrible loss which only someone who is utterly forsaken could feel. Herein is the horror of hell!

It all came to its terrifying climax on the cross when the Lord Jesus cried out with a loud voice, "My God, my God, why hast thou forsaken[deserted, abandoned] me?" We will never fully know what it meant for Him who knew no sin to become sin that in Him we might be made the righteousness of God (2 Cor. 5:21).

Somewhere in my past I developed the idea that at this time the holy Father turned His back on His own Son, because He could not bear to look upon a scene so evil and unholy. There is a sense of theological truth in this, but I fear the enemy has perverted the picture in our minds in a most grotesque way. (This is easily accomplished in the mind of an innocent child.) In our imagination we see the Father as turning His back and looking the other way just when His obedient Son needed His loving presence the very most. We then picture the heavenly Father treating us in the same way in our desperate hour of sin and need. How diabolical of Satan to so distort the redemptive plan of God!

It is true Jesus felt in full force the forsaken feeling that sin ultimately brings. But there is a misconception here that somehow the Father was not a part of the Son's suffering. I cannot accept this. Fellowship cannot be broken without both partners experiencing the pain. Furthermore, the Scripture says that God the Father was personally present in Christ reconciling the world to favor with himself . . . (2 Cor. 5:19, TAB). When the Father gave up His own Son for our redemption, He gave His very heart—there was something of the Father that went to the cross with Jesus. That is not a theological statement, but a simple conclusion based on the very nature of fatherhood. No earthly father can look upon his own son during a time of great sickness or sorrow and not feel an equivalent anguish in his own soul. How much more, then, did our heavenly Father feel for His beloved Son.

We earlier considered Abraham as one Old Testament type of the Father. Before coming across that illustration, I asked God to give me an example of a hurting father's heart that would help me to understand the pain which He experienced over the death of Jesus. I was almost immediately reminded of King David at the time of his son Absalom's death. Absalom had rebelled against his father and was seeking to take over the throne. (In one sense he becomes a type of Christ on the cross who took upon himself your rebellion and mine.) There was a reversal of Absalom's military fortune, however, and in his endeavor to escape on a mule, he was caught by his head in a tree (type of the cross?) where he was later slain by David's men.

When in time David was advised of his son's death, the sorrowful response of his father-heart is portrayed with great pathos:

> And the king was deeply moved, and went up to the chamber over the gate, and wept; and as he went, he said, O my son Absalom, my son, my son Absalom! Would God I had died for you, O Absalom, my son, my son! (2 Sam. 18:33, TAB)

We will never be able to fathom the agony of heart which our heavenly Father experienced when His beloved Son was placed upon the cross. How He would have spared His Son or even taken His place if such had been possible, but there was no other way. He did, however, fully and equally enter into the anguish and agony of that terrible hour.

Why was the heavenly Father willing to pay such a price for our redemption? It was because He loved us so. Can we ever again doubt the loving nature of our dear heavenly Father?

What About God's Wrath?

Where, some might ask, does the wrath and judgment of God fit into such a picture of the Father's love? Actually it takes the love of God to understand His wrath. God doesn't punish people for the cruel and perverted pleasure He might find in afflicting them with pain because of their rebellion. He is not motivated as are men by a desire for revenge or retaliation. Our heavenly Father by nature is not vindictive. We slander His character by so projecting our nature into His.

The Scriptures do declare that we are not to avenge ourselves, but to leave the way open for God's wrath; for it is written:

> Vengeance is mine, I will repay, says the Lord. . . .
> It is a fearful thing to incur the divine penalties and
> be cast into the hands of the living God! (Rom.
> 12:19, RSV; Heb. 10:31, TAB)

But the vengeance of God is derived from a New Testament Greek term that indicates a reaction which proceeds from a sense of justice whereby we fairly reap what we sow. It does not carry an undertone of vindictive self-gratification.

God's wrath has both direction and purpose. It flames forth towards anything and everything that has been selfishly or devilishly designed to separate us from His love. We reap what we sow that willful rebellion can be replaced by willful repentance. Or in the case of unpremeditated error, ignorance can be replaced by wisdom. In either case, God's discipline is designed with redemptive and corrective purpose in view, and is motivated by His love. The wrath of God has no meaning apart from His ultimate desire for a people who will worship Him in the beauty of holiness (Ps. 29:2).

The writer of the epistle to the Hebrews (who some scholars believe was Paul) persuasively presents the logic of love behind divine discipline:

> And have you forgotten the exhortation which
> addresses you as sons?—"My son, do not regard
> lightly the discipline of the Lord, nor lose courage
> when you are punished by him. For the Lord
> disciplines him whom he loves, and chastises every

son whom he receives." (Heb. 12:5-6, RSV)
Besides this, we have had earthly fathers to
discipline us and we respected them. Shall we not
much more be subject to the Father of spirits and
live? For they disciplined us for a short time at
their pleasure, but he disciplines us for our good,
that we may share his holiness. (Heb. 12:9-10, RSV)

One finds in the above passage an echo from the voice of
Isaiah concerning the ultimate purpose of Jehovah's
judgments:

O Lord, in distress they sought thee, they poured
out a prayer when thy chastening was upon them.
My soul yearns for thee in the night, my spirit
within me earnestly seeks thee. For when thy
judgments are in the earth, the inhabitants of the
world learn righteousness. (Isa. 26:16, 9, RSV)

The Ultimate Supremacy of the Father's Love

We discover the spirituality of the apostolic Church was
truly based upon a deep appreciation of the Father's
heart-desire for peculiar people—a royal family of beloved
sons and daughters—who, with their kingly Brother Christ
Jesus, would rule and reign with Him until all enemies would
be brought into subjection to His lordship. Paul states that
the last enemy to be destroyed is death (1 Cor. 15:21-26).

Then an amazing declaration is made concerning the
consummation of the ages: Everything will move into the
timelessness of eternity as it began, with the loving
supremacy of the Father himself.

When Christ has won his battle with all of his
enemies, then the Son himself will also become

subject to the Father, who gave the Son power over all things, that God may be all in all—everything to everyone everywhere! (1 Cor. 15:28, various versions)

As our spirits strain to even dimly glimpse something of the eternal glory of such divine fatherhood, we are left with a feeling of great humility, realizing we are but seeing as through a veil darkly. One feels the desire to tread softly when confronted with the timeless mysteries of God's divine plan for mankind. To dogmatize in rigid detail from our earthbound, timebound perspective can only lead to limitation and distortion of the truth.

The early church was characterized by an attitude of humility and flexibility concerning many of the divine mysteries in Scripture. Only in later years did Christian thought become more defined and dogmatic. This shift in mentality was related to the development of Western theology.

Western Versus Eastern Christianity

For some, theology is regarded as a highly sophisticated academic discipline which is restricted to spectacled scholars who reside in ivory towers totally detached from the real world. Because most of us consider ourselves a part of the real world, we fail to appreciate the powerful influence both positively and negatively which theology has had upon our attitudes about God and behavior towards man. There are very few people, if any, who can claim their concepts of Christianity have come solely from Scripture without any influence from traditional theology.

Just because we may not be aware of our religious roots does not minimize the effect they can have upon our basic attitudes. Sometimes a subconscious influence can be most pervasive and persistent in coloring or discoloring our whole perspective on life. Some people have lived most of their lives under a cloud of condemnation which they associate with a frowning father-image. Never once has it occurred to them that such an attitude about God may have developed early in their childhood when they were innocent victims of a very legalistic theology.

The early Eastern Church (Greek) held a Christian perspective far different than that which was to subsequently develop in Latin or Western Christianity. Eastern Christianity primarily viewed God as both the Father-Creator and Father-Redeemer of mankind. It was in His sovereign will and redemptive purpose to reclaim fallen man and his world as a matchless manifestation of His grace. Ultimately, God's love and truth in Christ Jesus would restore the ravages of sin and evil, and our heavenly Father would have a redeemed family who would ever worship and glorify Him. The emphasis was on God's redeeming love and sovereign power to accomplish His eternal purpose with and through His beloved family—beginning with our Redeemer-brother, the Lord Jesus. Though successive ages be involved, ultimately God's will would be accomplished here on earth as it had been planned in heaven. This would be the ultimate triumph of the Lord Jesus Christ, to the glory of the Father. Most of these basic tenets are held by the Eastern Orthodox Church of today. These early concepts are close in content and tone to what we already have found in the writings of the apostles in the first century.

Tertullian (AD 160-220) has been acclaimed as the father and founder of Western Christian thought. He was a brilliant orator, writer, and theologian in North Africa. He was the first to systematically explain the Scriptures in the Latin tongue of North Africa. Tertullian refused to translate

Greek theological terms, but created them in Latin and endowed them with his own personal bias. He was a lawyer of some renown, and excelled in framing formulas with clarity and precision. His legalistic background brought a highly juridical tone to his writings that featured God primarily as a legislator and judge. The emphasis was on the moral responsibility of man rather than the mercy of a forgiving Father. Man stands condemned before His divine magistrate, realizing he can never merit his own salvation. The primary response to such a God is one of fear, but of such proportions that His love and grace may sometimes seem beyond one's reach.

Robert Barr, a patristic scholar, summarizes Tertullian's position with this startling statement:

> In Tertullian, God becomes legislator and judge. God lays down a law and judges transgressors. Found guilty, the defendants must pay the penalty, unless after voluntarily entering a plea of guilty and appealing to the clemency of the court, they undertake to counterbalance the gravity of the penalty with an equal weight of virtuous actions. Some virtuous actions are commanded, others recommended; it is by the latter that the condemned pay their penalty.
>
> Does this sound familiar? It very well might, for a legalistic approach to broad areas of theology has remained characteristic of the Christian West since Tertullian inaugurated it in broad areas of his own theology in 200. Before then, and in the East even since then, such an approach was practically unheard of because it was unthought of. (*Main Currents in Early Christian Thought*, Paulist Press, 1966, p. 47)

It is recognized that a legalistic approach in certain aspects of Christian theology is legitimate, but in some Christian circles it has become a predominant theological mentality. For many the initial image of God as a merciless judge is so forceful, the portrait of the forgiving Father is completely obscured. Such individuals—many, sincere Christians—usually suffer from a supersensitive conscience and live under a continual cloud of condemnation, despite repeated pleas to God for forgiveness and grace. Satan has succeeded in deceiving them concerning the true nature of their heavenly Father.

We can summarize the basic extremes between Eastern and Western theology as follows:

Western Theology
1. Rational
2. Dogmatic
3. Structured
4. Responsibility (man)
5. Merits (man)

Eastern Theology
1. Mystical
2. Humility
3. Flexible
4. Sovereignty (God)
5. Mercy (God)

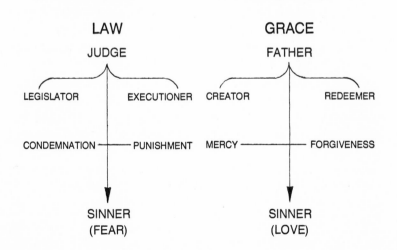

It is true, a holy fear of judgment for sin should lead us to godly sorrow and repentance, which then opens our lives to God's grace and forgiveness. Satan, however, seeks to pervert such holy fear into an attitude of hopeless condemnation. Wherever there is an emphasis on the legalistic elements of Christianity without a primary perspective built on the Father's love, the natural tendency will be towards an inner disposition of overriding fear and guilt. We then find it difficult to feel that we have ever been fully accepted by God, and are abiding in His loving approval. We have been victims of a theological extreme, and weren't even aware of its depressing influence on our lives.

No wonder Jesus said:

And ye shall know the truth, and the truth shall make you free. (John 8:32)

The setting for the above statement is most interesting. Jesus had just demonstrated the forgiving grace of God to the adulterous woman whom the Pharisees declared should be stoned to death as prescribed by Mosaic law.

The Pharisees then challenged Jesus concerning His relationship with the Father, and thereby lost the liberty His words—as God's Son and divine spokesman—could have brought to their lives. There is much sadness in such a scene, because it so clearly reveals the attitude and actions of a legalistic mentality. Pharisees of every age present a similar picture. Unaware of their own bondage, they seek to bring others into the captivity of a pernicious spirit of condemnation.

THE FATHERHOOD OF GOD IN THE EARLY CHURCH

What a welcome contrast we find in the gracious words of our loving Lord:

> So if the Son makes you free, you will be free indeed. (John 8:36, RSV)

4

Earthly Fathers Versus the Heavenly Father

The Father did not send His Son into just any family, but to Mary and Joseph who, as we have previously discussed, were loving, faithful, and grateful parents. Therefore little Jesus experienced the blessing of being a beloved, secure, and accepted son. Sadly, many cannot look back upon such a wholesome family relationship, because they were neither wanted, loved, nor appreciated.

Christ Jesus: Our Sympathetic Redeemer-Priest

The Scriptures declare that Jesus was tempted and tried in all points as ourselves, that He might become a high priest who has been touched with the feelings of our infirmities. He took upon himself the limitations of our humanity that He might sympathize with us in our sufferings, and thereby graciously help us in our time of need and affliction (Heb. 2:18; 4:15).

One might be tempted to wonder if Jesus can really identify with those who have had tragic family backgrounds since His childhood was so ideal. I was entertaining such questions in my mind on one occasion when it occurred to me that what our Lord did not personally experience in His life,

71

He did in His death, because He took upon himself the curse and full consequences of our sin that we might be restored to a wholesome and righteous relationship in the Father's family. Yes, Christ knows what it is to be hated, rejected, and forsaken. He can readily relate to us in our situations of suffering:

> Surely he has borne our griefs and carried our sorrows; yet we esteemed him stricken, smitten by God, and afflicted. But he was wounded for our transgressions, he was bruised for our iniquities; upon him was the chastisement that made us whole, and with his stripes we are healed. All we like sheep have gone astray; we have turned every one to his own way; and the Lord has laid on him the iniquity of us all. (Isa. 53:4-6, RSV)
> Christ redeemed us from the curse of the law, having become a curse for us—for it is written, "Cursed be every one who hangs on a tree"—(Gal. 3:13, RSV)
> He himself bore our sins in his body on the tree, that we might die to sin and live to righteousness. By his wounds you have been healed. For you were straying like sheep, but have now returned to the Shepherd and Guardian of your souls. (1 Pet. 2:24-25, RSV)

There is no tragedy of life with which Jesus is not already familiar; He is not only sympathetic, but redemptively empathetic. To sympathize (with+passion) with someone is to feel sorry for them in their need. To empathize (in+ passion) with someone is to enter into their pain with them. Jesus Christ as our Redeemer-brother not only felt sorry for the sinner and his suffering, but actually identified himself with both, that we might then also be one with Him in His resurrection life. Here is our hope and guarantee for healing in its broadest sense. What added meaning this brings to these familiar words of Jesus, "Go in peace (harmony of life) for your faith has made you whole."

Wholeness of life involves harmonious relationships with our heavenly Father, ourselves, and our brothers and sisters in Christ. We were not created to live empty, lonely lives apart from the loving fellowship of God's family. The Apostle Paul warmly describes our divine life relationship with the Father and His family in his letter to the Christians at Rome, who may have had some reason to feel somewhat isolated:

> And so we should not be like cringing, fearful slaves, but we should behave like God's very own children, adopted into the bosom of his family, and calling to him, "Father, Father." For his Holy Spirit speaks to us deep in our hearts, and tells us that we really are God's children. And since we are his children, we will share his treasures—for all God gives to his Son Jesus is now ours too. But if we are to share his glory, we must also share his suffering. (Rom. 8:15-17, TLB)

Obviously Satan would seek to limit our life in the Father's family by all possible means. We have seen how effectively certain legalistic extremes in Western theology have been subtly utilized to this end. Now we come to another approach which is just as sinister in its effect. It involves the perversion of our concept of divine fatherhood, by exploiting a variety of faulty earthly father relationships. It is very difficult to appreciate the fatherhood of God if we have no familiar earthly reference. Even worse are natural father relationships which are associated with serious emotional conflicts. Just the concept of fatherhood can create an almost insurmountable barrier in some people's approach to God.

We will now consider some of the various childhood relationships which the adversary would use to his advantage to cloud the true character of our heavenly Father. We will rely upon the ministry of our Blessed Comforter whom the Father has sent on our behalf that we might experience divine truth in love. Jesus referred to the Holy Spirit as the Spirit of Truth, but so tender and dove-like is His ministry of healing that we can expose our hearts and lives to Him without fear. Let us therefore confidently proceed in an attitude of faith, hope, and love.

The Fatherless Child

Some children have never known the love of an earthly father because of death, divorce, or desertion. Just a few days ago I talked to two Bible school students who deeply loved the Lord, but entertained poor images of their heavenly Father. The first was a girl whose concept of fatherhood was just a blank. "I never had a father; there is just nothing to remember." After counseling and praying for her, I then talked with a young man. His wife had just found a deep inner healing while listening to our series on the "Fatherhood of God," but he was still personally disturbed because of a similar need in his own life. He, too, had suffered the loss of an earthly father's attention and needed to feel the love and know the companionship of his heavenly Father. We prayed that God would make up for the lack of happy boyhood memories and experiences—the little boy who never went on a fishing trip with his dad, or played ball together in the back yard, or wrestled on the living room rug just for the fun of it. In an intimate and very touching way he laid his head on my shoulder as we allowed the Holy Spirit to heal and restore that part of his life that had waited for years to be warmed by a father's love.

What happened next really reached my heart, because the young lady I had prayed with earlier had patiently waited off to the side, since she needed a ride back to the dormitory. She was approaching us just as we rose, and I gave my young friend a final fatherly embrace. As I turned to recognize her presence, she looked up into my face—hesitated—and then wistfully said, "Could you give me a hug, too?"

I always feel a little tug at my heart when I see one of the current bumper stickers designed to be a gentle reminder to forgetful parents: "Have you hugged your kid today?" It is sad to realize that many kids will never receive the needed embrace from their father, because he has long since gone, and that loss will leave a lifetime scar.

My father died when I was three, and I have only a few childhood memories, reinforced by some faded photographs from an early family album. I recall once as a grown man feeling a very lonely sense of loss when I saw a picture of my father holding me as a child while I played in the sand at the beach. I also recall how apprehensive I was in grade school when we were scheduled to take a class in manual training. I felt all the other boys would have had experience using their fathers' tools, because I figured most of them had workshops in their garages or basements. I learned differently, of course, when the class began, but that hadn't helped during the previous weeks of anxious waiting. Then, too, there was the time the entire class laughed when we were making things in school for Mother's Day, because I had innocently asked if there was a day set aside for the fathers. Obviously, if you don't have a father, there is no Father's Day to celebrate.

I remember as an adolescent, reading the book of Proverbs, and explaining to God that I was going to take all of the passages that referred to sonship as His fatherly instruction to me personally. I discovered that our heavenly Father does indeed desire to fill the vacuum in the hearts of the fatherless with His love and counsel. But God went further than that, and herein lies an important truth. He also supplied me with an earthly father-figure during my early teen-age years. My Sunday school teacher took me under his wing, and we spent many hours together around my concerns and interests. It was he, who in spite of peril to life, limb, and property, patiently taught me to drive. I am sure there must be some special reward in heaven for such heroic endeavors.

The Need for Spiritual Fathers in the Family of God

Surely there is a practical principle here for us to receive, because I am convinced there are many unfulfilled people who are anxiously looking to the family of God for a "fatherly" ministry which their earthly family will never provide. Some desperately need to see, hear, and feel "the Word made flesh" all over again. Certainly this is one way the will of our heavenly Father can be accomplished here on earth as it is in heaven.

Sometimes such a fatherly ministry involves a relationship which extends over a period of time. I remember a black student of mine from overseas who was having some difficulty making adjustments to his new culture as well as the more rigorous routine of collegiate life. I prayed for and encouraged him on several occasions as he worked his way through his handicaps and difficulties. (He eventually went to graduate school and received a master's degree in public health.)

A few weeks before the end of the spring semester he

came to my office deeply disturbed, because he had heard we might not return to campus in the fall. I reluctantly informed him that we did feel God was leading us into another field of ministry. It was then that he confided in me that I had been a spiritual father to him in ways that went far beyond my level of awareness. He mentioned our times of prayer together, when he had been physically healed and released from serious depression. Often in lonely times at night he would recall encouraging words from our class devotions and find the consolation and comfort he needed.

It was with much sadness that we said goodbye, and after his departure, I paced the floor of my office deeply moved within. It was then that God assured me that such simple ministries to one of His dearest sons had come at a crucial period in his life when he desperately needed an earthly father-figure. I was then impressed that he had matured to such an extent that he was now ready to directly approach his heavenly Father with his needs. In time his privileges and responsibilities of divine sonship would include a ministry to others who would be coming to him for counsel and help. My fatherly ministry to him had come to an end, but his was about to begin.

On another occasion, the Lord accomplished a needed fatherly ministry in a matter of moments. I had finished a talk on the Father's love, and was waiting in the hotel lobby to be taken to the airport for my departure. A young lady in her teens or early twenties approached me, with tears in her eyes and wondered if I might have a moment to talk with her, because she desperately desired to know and feel the love of her heavenly Father. My heart sank within for I knew there was not time to counsel with her concerning all the underlying causes for her spiritual need.

In my desperation, I put my arm around her shoulder and simply said, "This is what I feel your heavenly Father wants to say to you: My dearest daughter, my heart goes out to you in love and compassion. When you are saddened, I am saddened; when you are grieved, I am grieved. You are very precious to me as a beautiful flower in my garden of love. I desire that you blossom and bloom in the delightful way in which I have made you. I myself, as your heavenly gardener, am watching over your life that it might bring beauty and blessing to others. You are a dear handmaiden in my beloved family, and it is my desire to forgive, heal, and restore you to the full joy of your divine daughterhood. I dearly love you with an everlasting love."

She burst into tears of heavenly joy, hugged me again and again, and went her way in the grace and peace of the Lord. It was all over in a moment, but I truly believe what her heavenly Father accomplished in that brief span of time will last a lifetime and beyond.

The Embittered Child

Sometimes the lack of an earthly father's care can lead to resentment the roots of which run deep within the subconscious soil of our hearts and minds. The last meeting of the conference had just concluded, and I had finished my teaching series on the Father-heart of God. The hour was late, but many remained for personal prayer and counseling. A young wife and mother waited with her husband until everyone else had left, then they, too, came to the prayer room for help.

The wife confessed she had cried during all of my messages throughout the three-day session, but didn't know why she was so deeply moved. There seemed to be an empty ache within her heart which she didn't understand. Her husband stood sympathetically by her side, obviously concerned for her emotional distress.

Her father had left her mother when she was too young to

remember. In fact, when we were involving our audience in the word-color associations, the term father to her was completely colorless. Her subconscious mind had totally blanked out any emotional response at this level.

Her mother never referred to her father in any way, but had endeavored herself to provide for her daughter as best she could. She recalled that her mother was usually too tired at the end of the day to give her the time and attention she wanted and needed and often raised her voice in emotional outbursts of personal frustration.

For a time they stayed at her grandmother's home where a makeshift bedroom was arranged in the dark and dreary recesses of the basement. Often she was required to go to bed alone while her mother was away for the evening. These were lonely and frightening experiences that were not appreciated by her adult world. She learned to withdraw within herself, and often found contentment in just being alone before the window watching the rain on the streets outside. It somewhat symbolized the peace she could experience by isolating herself from the disturbance afflicted upon her by unknowing loved ones.

Her mother remarried, but the new husband turned out to be more of a neutral friend, rather than a warm responsive father. She never knew what it was to be a loved and wanted daughter of an earthly father. She further confessed that she was happy to be a part of God's heavenly family, but could not feel that He looked upon her in any special or personal way. She was just one of many whom the Father loved in the great family of God. She saw herself as an unnoticed flower in a row of many flowers, contented she was even included in the garden.

I informed her that God had personally planted her in a very special way in His garden of grace. There was a particular place for her which the Father had planned, and

He had planted her husband by her side, with her children scattered nearby—a lovely and gracious setting of His choosing. She was in tears throughout our subsequent prayer, but confessed she still had the empty hurt in her heart, and really didn't want to recall unpleasant memories of the past. We again asked the Holy Spirit to go beyond our limitations, and reach the "little girl" of her emotions who wanted to be helped, but was afraid.

She then related a story—previously shared with her husband—of a very sad and tragic experience as a young girl when a family friend had cruelly abused and molested her. She had been afraid and ashamed to tell anyone of the experience for some time, but held the hurt within, until an ugly scar had been set within her soul. Although she had forgiven the man, subconsciously a mistrust of men in general had developed.

She honestly confided that on occasions such feelings—with related resentment—were even directed towards her husband whom she knew loved her very dearly. Moreover, she was sensing some of the same antagonism towards me although she was aware we both were sincerely and patiently trying to help her. It was then that the Holy Spirit lovingly exposed the root of her problem.

Much of the pain and hurt to which she had been exposed as a girl was due to thoughtless men. Because her father had deserted her, she not only missed the joys of young girlhood, but had been subjected to the disadvantages of a fatherless child. She had been disappointed, disillusioned, and degraded because of men. She was unable to give or receive love from her own dear husband as she needed because of a deeply rooted "male antagonism."

Without realizing it, this antagonism had also carried over to her relationship with her heavenly Father. He, too, was to be kept at arm's length. To fully submit to His will might only bring further disappointment and pain. He was to be loved and appreciated—but at a distance. It was safer just to be one of many flowers in a row, and receive the warmth of His love in a more general way.

At last the deception of the enemy had been discovered. His hidden hold was broken, and the healing process for the hurts of past years could begin. She immediately felt a deep peace of heart, and the empty ache was gone. Once more the Great Physician had faithfully ministered His healing power to a very dear daughter of God. Furthermore, as a handmaiden in the Father's royal family, she possessed the authority to maintain her peace of heart and freedom of mind. The Blessed Comforter himself had restored her soul, and she could rest in the meadows, or walk through the valleys without fear.

The Ignored Child

Even worse than the loss of an earthly father is the soul-scarring experience of having a father, but consistently being ignored. the lasting impression is one of worthlessness in personality. Years ago while ministering abroad in a Christian conference, I was impressed with the artistic talent of the pastor's wife. She was obviously an accomplished professional pianist. There was, however, a lack of warmth and joy in her appearance. In performance she was perfect, but there was a feeling of distance in her personality—a distance which bordered on loneliness. At first I thought it might have been the mark of personal detachment that some professionals develop, but subsequent events proved otherwise.

Following one of my teaching sessions on the fatherliness of God, her husband came to me and my wife with the urgent request that we pray with his wife who was weeping outside of the conference building. We seated ourselves on some nearby benches in the privacy of the park-like setting. After expressing our sympathetic understanding concerning her inner pain, we asked if our talk on the love of the Father had opened any scars from her childhood that the Lord lovingly wished to heal.

She responded by confessing that she never had felt truly loved or appreciated by her father. Most of the time he totally ignored her. Never had she heard him call her his "little princess" or any other term of intimate affection. Her relationship with her father was on his part one of personal indifference. The only time he showed any interest in her life was when she began to excel in her music. Then he would proudly display her talent, as one might wear a red feather in their cap.

In time she projected her father's attitude into everyone around her, including those associated with the church. She was sure their only interest in her was in what she could do for the church program, rather than what she was as a person. Consequently, she had learned to maintain a polite distance from people, insulating not only her life, but also her heart. This distance was also maintained in her relationship with her heavenly Father. She was careful to perform to perfection, and thereby obtain His paternal approval, but it was all very impersonal.

The revelation that God loved her just because she was His daughter was overwhelming. Even if she never played another note, she was assured the love of her heavenly Father would never be diminished. Tears of grief turned to joy as she became aware of her position as a beloved daughter in the family of God, and not beloved only of the Father, but very much loved and appreciated by her brothers and sisters in Christ. It was like watching a resurrection to see someone become alive to the love of God, after years of a lonely, loveless life without any hope for the joy which others seemed to experience. The dignity of divine daughterhood is indeed a priceless heritage.

The Unwanted Child

It is very difficult to imagine ourselves as bringing any joy or delight to our heavenly Father if all of our lives we have lived with the impression that we were "unwanted." To feel we arrived into this world as an unloved and unwanted "accident" is a horrible handicap under any circumstance. Only God's love can redeem such a tragic situation.

Sad stories with happy endings are always a joy to share. So often they begin with someone stating that although they know in their heads God is supposed to love them, they can't seem to feel it in their hearts. Such was the confession of a very serious and sad-faced teen-ager. After a little time of getting acquainted, I asked her if the Holy Spirit might bring some traumatic experience to her mind from the past that could have any bearing on her attitude toward her heavenly Father.

She immediately responded by relating how depressed she had become after learning that one of her girlfriends had undergone an abortion. She said she had cried for weeks, and was so saddened and grieved that there was an ache deep within her heart. There was no apparent connection, however, between this emotionally traumatic experience and her feeling about the Father.

I then inquired about her relationship with her own father, and the key to the whole situation was discovered. He had been very disappointed when she was born because he had really wanted a boy. When she was a youngster, she had acted like a tomboy to please her father—to be the boy he had always wanted.

As she grew into young womanhood, she had deliberately suppressed her developing femininity by refusing to wear frilly dresses or trying hair styles more befitting her maturity. It was then that the Holy Spirit revealed to her the cause of her great grief concerning her friend's abortion. Something deep within her cried out in sympathy, because she, too, knew what it was to come into this world unwanted and unloved.

The Holy Spirit responded at once with a personal word for her from the heavenly Father: "My dearest child, I want you to know that you were very much wanted when you came into this world, for you have been a part of my heart's desire from all eternity past. It was with divine expectation that you were born, and even greater joy when, through the Lord Jesus, you became a part of my family. You are a beloved child of mine in whom I find great pleasure. And, oh yes, my dear one, I just want you to know that I desired a daughter, and that is why I made you."

Her reaction was one of great relief and joyful release. At long last the great deception had been dispelled, and a very dear daughter knew without a doubt that she was wanted and loved by her heavenly Father.

The Threatened Child

A gifted Bible teacher once shared with me her unloved feeling with regard to the Father. She knew all of the right theology concerning her daughterhood in the divine family, but it wasn't as real in her heart as it was right in her head! The reason was rooted in her girlhood experiences. She was an only child of youthful parents. In their frustration over her childish disobedience and immaturity, they repeatedly threatened her to make her obey. Once they said they were going to give her away to the aborigines if she didn't obey. To prove their point, they packed her suitcase and dragged her down the front walk. She recalled she almost became hysterical with fear and begged to be given one more chance.

She was also told that if she didn't mind her father and mother, God would punish her for her disobedience. If she would fall and skin her knee or otherwise hurt herself, she was then informed this was the Father's way of punishing her as she had been warned.

Furthermore, she vividly remembered poring over an illustrated volume of Dante's *Inferno* where all the horrors of hell were devilishly detailed in a very grotesque fashion. Divine punishment was pictured as merciless torment without any purpose other than the divine pleasure which the endless agony of the doomed and damned would bring to a revenge-motivated Father-God.

These fearful impressions of God had so seared and scarred her subconscious mind that not even the balanced teaching of His grace in her adult years could heal the emotional trauma of her early girlhood. Her little girl heart still could not accept what her adult mind was affirming in a rational way. It took the deep inner-healing ministry of the Holy Spirit to assure the "little girl" of her emotional life that the Father was indeed a kind and forgiving person. The fearful Father image had to be replaced by the true picture of her loving heavenly Father.

One wonders how many other people have suffered for years in like fashion. I have discovered even Christian leaders—pastors, priests, missionaries, etc.—can still carry such hurts within their hearts despite having ministries blessed of God in many ways. What dreadful damage a legalistic theology can bring to God's own children.

As a young boy, I labored under the same delusion for years. I recall one occasion being sure I had crossed God's line of grace, and was forever lost with nothing but the literal fires of hell to look forward to. Finally I fell asleep from sheer emotional exhaustion. I have since discovered in sharing such experiences with Christian audiences the world over that sixty to seventy percent of God's people have felt at one time or another that they, too, had possibly crossed His line of grace, and He had given up on them.

An elderly pastor called me long distance on one occasion convinced that through a moral lapse in his life he had committed the unpardonable sin. His wife had forgiven him, and he had sincerely and sorrowfully repented before God, but could not feel that he was truly forgiven. It was as if he could not receive my counsel from Scripture or the testimony of my own experience. I finally rebuked the stubborn spirit of condemnation, and confessed on the authority of God's Word through the cleansing power of Christ's blood that he was free and forgiven—now and forever. I heard a shout on the other end of the line, and a song of spiritual praise and victory was lifted to the Lord with such enthusiasm, I don't think I would have needed the phone to realize what had happened. The Spirit of Truth had set another captive free.

Eternal life and eternal punishment are both derived from and conditioned by the timeless nature and character of God. How much wiser it is to leave the future ages in the hands of a holy, just, all powerful and ever-loving God rather than endeavoring to specifically define the heavenly and eternal scene by our earthbound, timebound minds. We can confidently trust all things into the care of our heavenly Father. Herein is our peace.

The Abused Child

Tragically many children have been physically abused or even sexually molested by their earthly fathers. I suspect the incidence of such abhorrent experiences is much higher than is generally thought. A woman in her fifties very bluntly confided in me that just to mention the word father brought only one image to her mind, which the reader can readily surmise. She had been repeatedly assaulted by her own father, who was a sadist. She also had been an unwanted child, delivered by a spiritualist, and had grown up in an atmosphere permeated with the occult.

Even though she had become a Christian and had been prayed for by many fellow Christians, she felt completely worthless, and even afraid of success in her life. She could neither receive nor give love to God, because even the thought of the Father filled her with strong feelings of revulsion. An inner voice warned her that she would die if she ever totally surrendered to the power of God's redeeming love.

I assured her it was God's love which had brought us together, and together we would acknowledge the lordship of our Christ. I then explained to her how the triumph of the cross had broken the power of the devil, who had sought to deceive her by afflicting her with threatening thoughts and painful memories of her tragic past. We confessed that Jesus was going to make her whole—spirit, soul, and body—so that she could be the handmaiden God had created her to be. No longer was she to see herself as a helpless, hopeless victim of evil powers, but a daughter of the King to whom was given power and authority over all the power of the devil.

Divine truth broke the hold of the adversary on her mind and emotions, and we confessed that the pure, holy light of God's love was bathing her inner being, and cleansing her from her unholy past. Satan was described as backing away and reluctantly bending his knee, bowing his head, and confessing the lordship of Jesus in her life. (This was a vision given to me once when praying for someone bound by fear.)

We claimed for the future that the concept of divine fatherhood was to convey feelings of a love which was clean, pure, and holy—a love which she could receive without reservation, and to which she could totally respond without fear. And respond she did—with tears of joy and relief. I then explained the principles by which she could continue her recovery, and resist the temptation to relapse to her original feelings. The enemy is a poor loser, but he has lost; therefore, our victory in the cross of Christ should be our constant confession. (*For additional thoughts on this theme, the reader is referred to the author's book*, Set My Spirit Free–*Logos International.*)

A part of our sister's healing in the above story was to realize how desperately sick her father had been. How very much he needed the forgiveness and deliverance that only God could bring to his life. As such perverted persons reach their later years, they sometimes begin to reap the remorse and regret which will only be intensified in their life beyond the grave. Again such agony over past sin is divinely designed to lead one to genuine repentance. If God is so gracious as to temper His justice with mercy, should we not allow His love to bring us to a place of prayer and forgiveness for those who have abused and mistreated us? How very desperately they need to be released from Satan's grip, and find the freedom which only the cross of Christ can bring. Such an attitude of forgiveness also releases us from the powers of resentment and bitterness. Such forces, if not rooted out by willfully submitting to the forgiving power of the Holy Spirit, can soon recapture our lives, and we again become prisoners of our past misfortunes. Praise God, the power which sets us free can keep us free if we continue to walk in the light of His love.

The Dominated Child

"Please pray that I might truly know the love of my heavenly Father, and experience the joy and freedom of divine sonship!" Such was the pathetic plea of a young man in his late teens or early twenties. He confessed that his father had been the perfect example of success: in athletics and academics, and later in various business ventures. Furthermore, he expected his sons to walk in his footsteps, and therefore persistently pressed them into his own mold. Over the years the young man became inwardly very resentful and frustrated by this dictatorial role which his father had assumed.

Sadly, his earthly father relationship was also discoloring his concept of his heavenly Father. He was beginning to feel that God was a divine dictator who could effectively force His will upon His helpless children with the threat of divine punishment. He really knew better, but the emotional impression was there.

He then explained that he finally had sought help through a deliverance ministry of exorcism. I inquired if this had been successful, and he indicated it had. (I felt uneasy in my spirit by his remark and wondered why he was still seeking help if his "deliverance" had been so effective.) I asked him how he knew he had been delivered. He said that while the man was exorcising him, he cried out with a loud voice.

"What did you say?" I asked.

"I yelled out, 'I hate that man! I hate that man!' " he replied.

"Who were you referring to?" I asked.

"I was referring to the man who was praying for me. He was pointing his finger at my face and repeatedly commanding the demon of witchcraft to come out of me."

A sudden thought crossed my mind and I expressed it to him in the form of a question: "Who did that man remind you of?"

The boy paused as if startled by such a question, and with amazement written on his face, he exclaimed, "Why, he reminded me of my father!"

I then shared with him what I had discerned within. In seeking demonic deliverance, he had been placed in an emotionally charged situation, in which all of the inner pressures of hostility and resentment toward his father had finally boiled over. All it took was the demanding, shouting, finger-pointing, father-figure image of an exorcist to trigger the whole scene.

I explained to him that rather than demonic deliverance, I earnestly felt that God wanted to bring him into an experience of inner healing that would help him to understand his feelings and explosive behavior.

First, I pointed out that of all people his own father had some serious spiritual needs. Anyone who so compulsively would strive to dominate his children and force his own life style upon them must have some deep feelings of inferiority or insecurity. Success, which is achieved by the driving force of compulsion, does not speak of a soul which is at peace with itself or with the world—let alone God. It was important for him to understand his father, and not hold feelings of resentment or hostility toward him. God could give him the power to love, forgive, and pray for his father's innermost needs.

Secondly, in the process of forgiveness, God would heal the hurts of his own heart, so no lasting scars would hinder his own personal development. Furthermore, the heavenly Father would assure him that the most precious part of selfhood was his will. Only creatures of choice can truly love and worship God. Both love and worship by their very nature must be spontaneously expressed; neither can be forced.

Our heavenly Father does have a plan and purpose for our lives, but it is one that brings fulfillment, not frustration. Only as we first submit to the delight of God's will can He then give us the desires of our hearts (Ps. 37:4). What a wonderful privilege is ours to be obedient sons and daughters of such a wise and loving heavenly Father.

I remember as we expressed these thoughts in prayer, he spontaneously laughed and cried, hugging me over and over again. Once more a dear son had found his Father, and a Father had found His son. I guess only heaven will fully reveal everything that happens on such a holy and beautiful occasion. We do sense something of the divine wonder, however, deep within our spirits.

The Pampered Child

Some children, far from being dominated, have their every wish and whim immediately gratified by indulgent parents. Their image of fatherhood is as spoiled as they are. They are spared the responsibilities of work and household chores. Never are their wills crossed, because concessions are always made in their favor. Under the guise of fatherly love they are showered with gifts far beyond their needs or wants. They can wheedle their own way regardless of parental preferences. Such indulgence often is derived from a parent's fear of displeasing the child, and thereby losing his love and respect. A spirit of intimidation prevails, and instead of the father presenting a picture of fairness and firmness, he is looked upon as a doting "sugar daddy."

A steady diet of candy-coated compliments soon convinces little John or Mary that there is no one as bright, talented and attractive as they are. If indeed they are so favorably endowed, they may even attain adulthood laboring under a serious misconception of what mature, responsible sonship and daughterhood truly involves—on both earthly and heavenly levels. For others a very rude awakening sometimes occurs when they are confronted with the unvarnished reality of school, work, or marriage.

The greatest harm, however, can be the misconception they may develop concerning their heavenly Father. They never move beyond the childish level of seeing God only as the divine supplier of their wants and wishes. Prayer becomes a perpetual presentation of personal needs and problems. Such spiritual selfishness can only lead to leanness of soul. Perhaps more tragically, when they begin to reap what they have sown in both attitudes and actions, their image of the heavenly Father can be totally shattered. Improper and unanswered prayers then lead to doubt and despair.

I know of one lady whose life of indulgence brought repeated tragedy even into her later years. A series of broken marriages, physical reversals and other personal misfortunes convinced her the Father was neither loving nor forgiving. Yet, through it all the heavenly Father was patiently waiting for her to come to her senses that she might find her way back into His beloved family where the healing powers of repentance and obedience could restore her self-mutilated life. How differently the story might have been if she had only known the firm, but loving hand of an earthly father.

The Unloved Child

"Would you please take time to pray and counsel with a friend of mine who desperately needs someone to help her?"

I had just finished speaking on the love of the Father, and was standing outside the door to the conference hall. The foyer was crowded with people coming and going, and the usual confusion of many voices somehow reminded one of the crowded marketplaces that Jesus used to visit. Yet, He always had time for the individual in need, and it seemed as if His Spirit was leading in that direction this very moment.

"She is waiting for us right over there by the drinking

fountain." My youthful guide led me through the maze of people to Cindy, who looked strangely lonely in such a large crowd. After introducing me, our young friend excused herself to find an older woman who was a special friend to both of the girls. They wanted her to be included in our conversation.

Cindy was a young woman perhaps in her early twenties. She immediately began to confess her uncertainty concerning our suggested prayer time. "I am so confused and mixed up inside," she said. "I don't know if God cares any more, or if I even want to seek His help." Then she proceeded to share with me how very unhappy her life was, and to make matters worse, her mind was continually plagued by unclean thoughts. Her words of reservation, however, were not at all in harmony with the pathetic plea for help that I could see in her eyes.

At that time the other two ladies arrived on the scene. Almost immediately the older woman in all sincerity pointed her finger at Cindy and reminded her that her first course of action was to repent if she expected to receive anything from the Lord. I didn't feel in my spirit that this was exactly the point where God wanted to enter the scene, so I suggested we leave the noisy hallway and find a quiet place where we could peacefully talk without being disturbed. We confessed together that Jesus would very much be a part of our conversation and that we would trust His Holy Spirit to direct our thoughts, words, and feelings.

I then shared with Cindy that my father had died when I was very young, and how I had subsequently developed a very distorted concept of what the love of our heavenly Father was truly like. I further explained that many times I had been paralyzed by fear and guilt, but had finally come to understand how great is God's grace, and how deep is the love of our forgiving Father.

She then confided in us that as a little girl her own father was only home on weekends because of his work. Then it seemed she had to compete with her mother and two brothers for his love and attention. She shared some specific memories in this regard that sadly illustrated her point.

In her very early years she found the extra love and consideration she needed from her grandfather. He was very devoted to his granddaughter and took time to play games with her, or just hold her in his lap and talk. It was a great loss for her when grandfather died, because his place in her heart and life was very special.

She discovered, however, a very kindly neighbor gentleman who likewise gave her the attention and support she needed. She recalled the many times they walked and talked together while watching the squirrels and listening to the birds in the trees. Here, again, she had discovered someone who would take time to share his life with her.

However, as she entered her teen years, the family moved, and she never again found the father-figure she needed and wanted. Instead she turned to the unreal world of fantasy and fiction. She became an avid reader of romantic novels, which in content were far beyond her level of emotional maturity. This was how she became a victim of the unclean thoughts which she had earlier confessed. Without realizing it, she was still trying to fill a void in her life which only God's love could satisfy.

Her teacher learned of her reading habits and notified her mother. They both confronted and condemned her for her wicked ways and evil habits. She said she knew they were partly right, and she felt very guilty, but at the same time she experienced a deep sense of resentment and rebellion—an inner attitude that had remained unchanged. I asked her how she felt her heavenly Father looked upon her life, and she confessed that He was probably very angry and disappointed, and she couldn't blame Him for turning His back on her.

By now, of course, the picture had become very clear. Basically she was a very affectionate person and needed the love and security that a healthy family life should bring. Lacking this, she had turned elsewhere. At each turn, however, she sooner or later suffered further loss and frustration. We helped her understand her feelings, and assured her that God wanted to heal her life within, and provide the loving support she needed from her heavenly Father.

It is one thing, however, to expose an inner need of the heart, and another to reach it with God's healing love. Words alone will not suffice; it takes the gifts and graces of the Holy Spirit himself. No wonder He is called our Blessed Comforter. The Lord reminded me of a vision which a lady had shared with me concerning her need to personally know the love of the Father. Developing that theme I asked Cindy to close her eyes and follow along in her imagination a scene which the Holy Spirit desired for her to see.

I suggested that she picture the Lord Jesus standing by her side as her loving Redeemer-brother. As His little sister, she could look directly into His face and make the delightful discovery that he was already looking down upon her. Furthermore, she would immediately notice His expression of loving care and concern. She could feel the strength and security of His presence, and also sense the peace and quiet joy that comes with the inner assurance that He would never leave.

Jesus was then seen as taking her hand as they walked along, admiring the beauty and wonder of their Father's world. She just knew there was nothing they couldn't talk about, because He seemed to understand everything—even if she had difficulty trying to put her innermost thoughts and feelings into words. It was comforting to know there was someone who knew her even better than she knew herself. So, they walked and talked together.

After a time she became aware that the Lord was actually taking her somewhere—and intuitively she knew—they were going to Father's house. Upon entering the door, Jesus took her directly into the presence of the Father himself. He was seated in a chair as if waiting for their arrival. His hands were open and extended upon His lap. Jesus then took both of her hands in His, and brought her to the Father, where He placed her hands in those of the Father.

Immediately she was drawn close to Father's heart, where she could cradle her head upon His shoulder, and feel the loving caress of His arms as she securely rested in His embrace. Very little needed to be said, because His eyes were filled with forgiveness and compassion, and she knew that everything was all right. He had never turned His back upon her, and she could have readily come to Him ever so much earlier, because her own dear heavenly Father had been waiting just for her.

By now Cindy was laughing and crying for joy. I have never seen a face so bright and beautiful, because with the tears was a smile of assurance. She would never be alone again; she had found her heavenly Father at last!

We left Cindy with one last word of counsel concerning the tactics of the tempter. "Don't be surprised if on some holy occasion an unholy thought comes racing through your mind. The adversary is a poor sport, and may well throw a few more punches after the final bell has sounded. Immediately bring Jesus into the scene, and simply inform Him that you know He saw the thought, too, and neither of you plan to give it the time of day."

There is divine purpose in that little illustration: It prevents us from unwittingly chain-reacting the thought into an unwholesome fantasy in one direction, or into guilt feelings in the other direction, which would soon smother us under a cloud of condemnation. Just the confessed presence of Jesus cuts the thought on both ends, and like a rootless, leafless seed, it will wither and die.

Lessons From Life

From the many illustrations considered thus far in our writing, I think it becomes apparent that problems often have a variety of causes. Man has a tendency to want to simplify and reduce the ministry of the Holy Spirit to a series of quick-answer formulas that will assure him of a perpetual ministry of success. It doesn't take any honest counselor very long to realize that, although we may learn certain principles by which personal problems are faced, ultimately it takes the discernment and ministry of the Holy Spirit to reach their roots with God's releasing power!

Christ is the answer! There is no other, because God has chosen to speak to the needs of mankind through His only Son. However, it takes the ministry of the Holy Spirit to make the answer practical and personal. We can never realize God's ultimate purposes in our lives apart from the Holy Spirit.

We also need to realize that some problems are derived from our own sinful ways. For these difficulties, we are to blame. Our response should be one of repentance, and turning to Jesus as our Brother and Redeemer. The blood of Jesus can never cleanse us from sins which are ignored, excused, or rationalized away. Only sins which are confessed can be rid of their guilt-producing power (1 John 1:9).

Other distressing situations, however, stem from willfully indulging in the weaknesses of the flesh (old sin nature) until they develop into a persistent habit-pattern. We begin with the idea that we can "take it or leave it," only to find in time we have been taken and we can't leave it. Again, we are responsible and will only find victory as we rely upon the power of the Holy Spirit to crucify our old nature. Don't try it alone—this provision comes to us through Jesus as our sanctifying Brother.

Some areas of need in our lives are not related to problems for which we are directly responsible. We have touched on several situations already. Guilt derived from an extreme theology of legalism will never be remedied by much confession or self-crucifixion. It requires the ministry of inner healing, which only Jesus, our Great Physician, can bring.

Likewise, individuals bound by Satan or demonic powers have problems which repentance, crucifixion, or inner healing won't reach alone. They need to be released through the power of the Holy Spirit, which again comes from Jesus our mighty Deliverer.

Often a combination of these four components may contribute to a complex problem. Repentance, crucifixion, healing, and deliverance may all be involved in the remedy. We need to assume responsibility for whatever part of the problem is really ours, but expect and claim God's healing and deliverance for what is not.

Fortunately, Jesus is the answer, whatever the cause, and if we are sensitive to the diversity of ministry provided by the Holy Spirit, we can discern the next step. Even the steps come in no fixed sequence. In the case of Cindy, she first needed healing of a faulty father-image. How could she receive forgiveness from a heavenly Father she felt had already turned His back on her? The story of Jesus leading her to the Father brought healing and probably deliverance. The counsel concerning how to face further temptation was actually teaching on the sanctifying power of the cross. That part of her old nature would lose its strength and die as she persistently proclaimed the power of Christ's Spirit in her life as a beloved daughter in the royal family of God.

To be aware of the possible approaches to personal problems will keep us from becoming one-shot ministers. As mentioned before, there is a natural tendency to oversimplify complex situations. Following this narrow set of mind, every inner conflict is due to unconfessed sin. Consequently, repentance is the only solution. Or, all personal problems are rooted in the old sin nature and, therefore, the answer is found only in self-crucifixion. Still others may put all their eggs in the basket of deliverance. Every disturbance is seen as demonic in origin and, therefore, requires an exorcism. And, of course, some of us would tend to lump every need under the heading of inner healing and proceed to probe into the past for subconscious emotional roots. Again, how very dependent we are upon the Holy Spirit to bring the kind of wholeness which Jesus faithfully ministered. Then we, too, can say, "Go in peace."

We can summarize the balanced approach needed for a ministry of wholeness as follows:

PROBLEM COMPONENTS

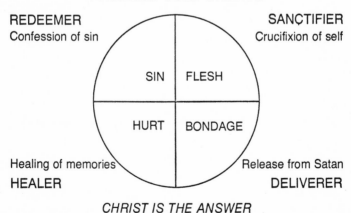

REDEEMER
Confession of sin

SANCTIFIER
Crucifixion of self

SIN | FLESH

HURT | BONDAGE

Healing of memories
HEALER

Release from Satan
DELIVERER

CHRIST IS THE ANSWER

5

Why Did My Heavenly Father Let It Happen?

"My God, if you don't care any more, then I don't either!"

With that an anguished mother cursed her heavenly Father to His face! There was an immediate response from God himself, and herein lies a story most worthy of our consideration.

The entire account was related to me by a middle-aged lady who thought others might profit from her experience. She had persistently worked and prayed to maintain the spiritual welfare of her home under some very difficult and desperate conditions. She had striven almost to the breaking point to hold everything together as a faithful wife and mother. Then it happened.

She was in the kitchen when she received the soul-shattering news that her fourteen-year-old daughter had become pregnant. Everything broke within her heart and all of the hurt, frustration, and resentment exploded heavenward towards God in whom she had previously placed her trust. Following all of the other painful events of her immediate life, why had the Lord allowed this to happen? If this is what the heavenly Father is truly like, He is not worthy to be praised, only to be cursed.

What happened next is most remarkable. She said she heard God speak to her and these were His words: "My dearest daughter, I have waited a long time for you to come to the place where you would receive all of my love for you."

She then confessed that it was as if she laid her head in the lap of her heavenly Father and wept for almost half an hour. "From that time to this, I have never once doubted God's great love for me." She then encouraged me to share this story with others who might at any time be tempted to think that God didn't love or care for them any longer.

Some of us might have been surprised by the tender, loving response of the Father to someone who had just cursed Him to His face. The answer is very simple: God understood her pain and frustration, and fully realized she wasn't really cursing Him, only what she thought He was like, and He wasn't like that at all.

Still, some might say if the Father is almighty and loving, why would He allow His children to suffer such pain and disappointment. Here is a mother who had faithfully been praying that God would protect and heal her home and family. Was all of this God's will? And if it was not, why did it happen? Was it a lack of faith in her own life? Why? Why? Why?

It Was My Fault That My Daughter Died

I am reminded of another grief-stricken mother who, for three years since the death of her daughter, had been unable to praise or worship her heavenly Father. It wasn't due to bitterness or resentment in her heart towards God, but a great feeling of guilt, because she felt she had not been able to exercise enough faith to effect a healing of her daughter's cancer. I explained to her that divine healing was not an end in itself, but always related to God's ultimate purpose, which goes far beyond our earthly and temporal sense of values.

For this reason faith cannot be reduced to a formula that leaves both the control and responsibility in our hands. There are some questions related to the heavenly realm that will never be answered within the framework of our earthly mentality. It takes an eternal perspective to see beyond the limitations of the present.

I asked her if she remembered how the mighty prophet Elijah had been transported to heaven. She recalled it had been a rather dramatic departure involving a spectacular whirlwind, a chariot, and horses of fire. I then asked if she knew how his successor, Elisha—the man of double-portion power—had been taken home, and of this she had no recollection. Elisha was indeed a mighty man of faith with many more miracles recorded in his ministry than Elijah. His departure, however, was something less than sensational. Perhaps this is the reason it never made the list of selected stories for children's Sunday school lessons.

You might be interested to read the account from Scripture. "Now when Elisha had fallen sick with the illness of which he was to die . . . so Elisha died and they buried him" (2 Kings 13:14, 20, RSV). The account hardly seems worthy of recording—a mighty man of faith falling sick with a terminal illness in his old age. This is certainly something far short of the glorious gateway one might expect would have been such a prophet's entrance to his heavenly home.

Many might even question if in his declining days he had lost some of his faith and power. Yet we are told he was prophesying right to the end (vv. 14-20). Furthermore, we are informed that some time later when a marauding band of Moabites surprised a local funeral procession, the pallbearers in their haste to escape, unceremoniously dropped the corpse into Elisha's grave. Upon touching Elisha's bones, the man revived and leaped to his feet (vv. 20-21). Seemingly, Elisha had retained enough power in his

103

bones to energize an unsuspecting corpse.

Perhaps there is a lesson here. God's ways and our ways do not always coincide. There are dimensions in God's will that defy man's comprehension. One thing we can comprehend, however, is that God loves us without reservation. I assured this grief and guilt-stricken mother that her heavenly Father dearly cared for her. He had been saddened by her loss, and wished to comfort and console her himself. We may not understand all of the mysteries of divine healing in a physical sense, but it was most assuredly His will on this occasion to heal her wounded heart. Following a brief prayer of deliverance and assurance, she burst into a spiritual song of praise and worship. Once again a dear daughter of God had been released from a heavy cloud of condemnation and brought back into the divine peace which is the privilege of Father's beloved children.

Suffering: Its Source and Sanctification

Still, the question can persist. Why does God allow His children to suffer if He truly loves them? It is necessary to understand both God's nature and ultimate purpose to face such a question from His perspective. God created man in His own image. Because God is sovereign and unique, there is a measure of sovereignty and individuality with which man is endowed. This enables him to personally love and worship God, because both functions by nature must be spontaneous (spring from our free will). Neither can be forced, as mentioned earlier.

Man was also given dominion and authority over the natural order of creation.

> And God blessed them, and God said to them, "Be fruitful and multiply, and fill the earth and subdue it; and have dominion over the fish of the sea and

104

over the birds of the air and over every living thing
that moves upon the earth. (Gen. 1:28, RSV)
When I look at thy heavens, the work of thy
fingers, the moon and the stars which thou hast
established; what is man that thou art mindful of
him, and the son of man that thou dost care for him?
Yet thou hast made him little less than God, and
dost crown him with glory and honor. Thou hast
given him dominion over the works of thy hands;
thou has put all things under his feet. (Ps. 8:3-6,
RSV)

In one sense there was a risk involved. Should such divine
privilege and power be abused, the entire realm of creation
would suffer. We know the sad story, because man did
debase his holy position and surrendered to Satan his
God-given authority by yielding to the deceptive promise of
self-realization apart from the will of his Father-Creator. He
thereby disinherited himself from God's family, and brought
the whole order of creation under the curse of his sin. No
longer do we live in a world of perfect peace and harmony.
That divine balance has been destroyed, and we see the
harsh extremes which prevail in our natural world. Many of
the so-called acts of God are really the results of a creation
that lost its original character when its rightful sovereign
(man) fell from his place of divine dominion.

God was not caught off-guard, however, by man's
rebellion, because redemptive purpose had been built in to
creation's plan. Through Christ Jesus, their
Redeemer-brother, a royal family is still destined to reign in
the kingdom of God. Under Christ their king, divine order in
every realm will be restored as true sons and daughters
fulfill the will of their heavenly Father throughout all ages to
come:

In my opinion, whatever we may have to go through now is less than nothing compared with the magnificent future God had planned for us. The whole creation is on tiptoe to see the wonderful sight of the sons of God coming into their own. The world of creation cannot as yet see reality, not because it chooses to be blind, but because in God's purpose it has been so limited—yet it has been given hope. And the hope is that in the end the whole of created life will be rescued from the tyranny of change and decay, and have its share in that magnificent liberty which can only belong to the children of God.

It is plain to anyone with eyes to see that at the present time all created life groans in a sort of universal travail. And it is plain, too, that we who have a foretaste of the Spirit are in a state of painful tension, while we wait for that redemption of our bodies which will mean that at last we have realized our full sonship in him. We were saved by this hope, but in our moments of impatience let us remember that hope always means waiting for something that we do not yet possess. But if we hope for something we cannot see, then we must settle down to wait for it in patience. (Rom. 8:18-25, Phillips)

As clearly indicated in the above passage, redemptive purpose is not yet complete. It begins in the hearts of God's people who, regardless of circumstances, commit themselves to His love and wisdom. We still live in a world which suffers from the curse of self-willed man. But by expressing God's love and life to others, we can become a light of hope and a promise for better things to come. We can present an alternative that has the power to leaven society itself. Not all will respond to the light of God's love in our day, as was true in the day of Christ. But there is the promise of a witness to the very ends of the earth. Then shall come the end—or should we say the beginning—because this is the hour when Christ will return, and His kingdom shall be established here on earth!

> And as he sat upon the mount of Olives, the disciples came unto him privately, saying, Tell us, when shall these things be? and what shall be the sign of thy coming, and of the end of the world? [And Jesus answered] And this gospel of the kingdom shall be preached in all the world for a witness unto all nations; and then shall the end come. (Matt. 24:3, 14)

In the meantime God will not directly impose His righteousness upon the wicked affairs of sinful man and thereby violate the limited sovereignty of man's will. We should not blame God for the evil consequences of sinful man in our world. Even the violent tragedies of nature—so-called acts of God—can ultimately be traced back to the results of man's original rebellion.

However, God can through the power of His Spirit weave the evil designs of sinful men with the prayers and actions of the righteous to ultimately bring forth His divine purpose. Man can only go so far before his sin works against him. The same is true for society. As history records, whole civilizations have risen and fallen in line with this divine principle. Just because God does not impose His will upon man as one would play with a puppet does not mean He is not ultimately in control, but His purpose involves a process that includes a people of faith, love, and obedience.

As Christians we are not guaranteed immunity from all of the consequences of living in a world disordered at every level by man's sin. However, we do have the promise that everything can be sanctified by God's redeeming Spirit to bring forth a family for the Father whose life and nature will be in the image and character of the Lord Jesus Christ. Absolutely nothing can happen to us within or without that God will not use to make us more like Jesus and fit us for our place in His royal family.

The Good Toward Which All Things Work

As one who has experienced the truth that he proclaims, Paul emphatically presents this tremendous theme of God's perfecting power in these remarkable words:

> Moreover we know that to those who love God, who are called according to his plan, everything that happens fits into a pattern for good. God, in his foreknowledge, chose them to bear the family likeness of his Son, that he might be the eldest of a family of many brothers. (Rom. 8:28-29, Phillips)

Now God does protect His children from many of the accidents and adversities in life. All of us can recall situations where one second, or one inch was all there was between us and tragedy. We could almost hear the rustle of the angels' wings as we recognized it was God's guarding hand which preserved our lives. On other occasions we have not been spared the darkened skies and stormy seas of suffering and trial. But in time God did deliver us from our sickness, restore us from financial loss, or heal some breach in a personal relationship. And, we gave Him much praise for stilling the storm and returning us to our haven safe and sound. But God's redemptive purpose often goes beyond just protection and deliverance.

For what God does not:
protect us from, or
deliver us out of, He will
perfect us through.

That perfection—that good towards which all things work—is nothing less than the very life of Jesus Christ himself. There is no circumstance in life, nor weapon of Satan's design, which in God's hand will not ultimately work for our good and God's glory.

We are so conditioned to measuring success in terms of earthly, temporal values that we fail to appreciate that God's yardstick relates to an entirely different realm. Time is important only in the light of eternal purpose. Earthly pleasure and profit have meaning only as they express and contribute to God's heavenly kingdom. We say the words so easily until we are forced by circumstances to commit ourselves to one standard or the other.

What She Feared Came Upon Her

After I had spoken about the reality of heaven and the on-going purposes of God for our lives after death, a young mother expressed her appreciation in a most sincere and personal way. I had mentioned that because there was a "man" in the heavens—the Lord Jesus himself—we had a guarantee that heaven would not be so unearthly that there would be no familiar frames of reference whatsoever. Everything that is beautiful, noble, and lovely in this life will have its extension in the next, but without the limitations that sin has brought to our earthly existence. I also indicated that our individuality would be retained, but undergo development as God's creative Spirit conformed us into the infinite wonder of Christ's likeness.

Then she explained that she had recently lost her five-year-old son and was so comforted to realize that he would continue to grow and develop as the little person she knew him to be. But, there was much more to the story than this, and it helps bring the lofty truths previously shared down to earth in a personal and practical way.

She had recently read a book which emphasized the need for each one of us to come to our "Gethsemane" and, like Jesus, to totally surrender our wills to God. As we have previously discussed, the adversary will so pervert the truth that the life and liberty that it can bring is not only lost, but distorted in such a way as to bring bondage and death. The very thought of surrendering everything to God chilled her heart with intense fear. She was sure that if she fully yielded to God's will, He would require her to surrender the life of her little son--probably a warped carry-over from a Sunday school story of Abraham and Isaac.

She finally decided in all honesty that she could not make this kind of a commitment to God. Five days later her little son was dead! An ice-cream truck, while backing up, had accidentally run over her little boy, crushing him to death. What words of comfort could one give a grief-stricken mother under such circumstances? How totally helpless anyone would feel apart from the faithful ministry of the Holy Spirit—our Blessed Comforter!

Destined to Bloom in Heaven

I truly sensed His presence, and emphatically assured her that this tragedy was not from the hands of an angry God who, because of her reluctance to submit to His will, was acting from an attitude of vengeance. Rather, in this tragedy, the heavenly Father desperately wanted her to come to Him for consolation. He, too, knew what it was to lose a Son, and great was His concern for her—a beloved daughter who was suffering the pain only she and God could understand.

The Father assured her that her little son was in His loving hands, and indeed, while he had been planted in the garden of her love for only a short time, that little boy was destined to bloom in heaven and become the noble person God always intended him to be.

Divine Recovery with a Purpose

Furthermore, God wanted to make it up to her by not only easing the pain of her loss, but during her time of recovery He wished to reveal more of His love for her. She, in turn, could then be used to comfort others in their time of affliction, for her heart would be particularly sensitive to their need. Yes, all of us are drawn closer to the Lord during times of tragedy, but also to each other in the family of God.

Surely this was what Paul was referring to when, from his heart, he wrote these words so filled with feeling and personal understanding:

Thank God, the Father of our Lord Jesus Christ, that he is our Father and the source of all mercy and comfort. For he gives us comfort in our trials so that we in turn may be able to give the same sort of strong sympathy to others in theirs. Indeed, experience shows that the more we share Christ's suffering the more we are able to give of his encouragement. This means that if we experience trouble we can pass on to you comfort and spiritual help; for if we ourselves have been comforted we know how to encourage you to endure patiently the same sort of troubles that we have ourselves endured. We are quite confident that if you have to suffer troubles as we have done, then, like us, you will find the comfort and encouragement of God. (2 Cor. 1:3-7, Phillips)

Yes, we may not always be spared some of the suffering which is the lot of mankind—any more than Jesus was—but we will always have the full measure of love which the Father has for His children during their time of affliction. Furthermore, God promises to redeem our pain and adversity. Nothing will be lost or wasted. Everything can be utilized for our ultimate good and His greater glory.

If we were spared all of the pain and affliction which is the lot of this sin-cursed world, we would never develop a true sense of compassion for others, nor could they relate to us as a source of help and healing. There would be no common ground for sympathetic—yes, even empathetic—understanding

Affliction: The Ground From Which the Flower of Compassion Grows

There is a sense in which we can share in—not add to—Christ's sufferings, and thereby be assured that we also shall share in the ministry of life which such suffering brings to birth. From the harsh ground of affliction blooms the fragrant flower of compassion.

My boyhood pastor once related to me the story of a noted healing evangelist of many years ago. He was a man of integrity and commitment. So strong was his conviction concerning the doctrine of divine healing for all who would believe that his family never relied upon medicine of any kind. There wasn't an aspirin tablet to be found in their travel trailer. God honored this simple man of faith, and his healing ministry was blessed throughout the country. He had very little patience, however, with people who wavered in their faith. It almost bordered on an attitude which implied that if they didn't have enough faith to be healed, they deserved to be sick.

On their way to my pastor's church for a series of meetings, they experienced an accident on the highway, and the evangelist suffered a serious injury to one of his legs. For days he refused medication of any kind, until the doctors were gravely concerned because the infection was spreading. My pastor finally faced him with the seriousness of the situation, and asked him how he felt about the matter. His reply was prompt and emphatic, "I am resisting the devil!" My pastor then reminded him that there was a prior condition—and attitude of heart—that preceded that exhortation. The entire passage reads:

> God gives strength to the humble, but sets himself against the proud and haughty. So give [submit] yourselves humbly to God. Resist the devil and he will flee from you. (James 4:6-7, TLB)

The Apostle Peter reaffirms this thought with these words of admonition:

> Humble yourselves therefore under the mighty hand of God, that in due time he may exalt you. Cast all your anxieties on him, for he cares about you. Be sober, be watchful. Your adversary the devil prowls around like a roaring lion, seeking some one to devour, Resist him, firm in your faith, knowing that the same experience of suffering is required of your brotherhood throughout the world. And after you have suffered a little while, the God of all grace, who has called you to his

eternal glory in Christ, will himself restore, establish, and strengthen you. To him be the dominion for ever and ever. Amen. (1 Pet. 5:6-11, RSV)

My pastor then pressed the point, "Dad, what are you trying to prove, and to whom are you trying to prove it?" Rigidity in doctrine can sometimes lead us to a proud, unloving spirit. "Dad" finally submitted to the doctor's skills and medication as unto the Lord. Two things happened in the subsequent weeks. A perverse, foul-mouthed man in an adjacent room was beautifully brought into the family of God through dad's testimony. And, secondly, his subsequent ministry to the sick took on a new dimension—an attitude of patient, loving, compassion. Submitting in the Lord to suffering had wrought a change in his character—eternal in nature—which a lifetime of hard-line faith teaching had failed to produce. No wonder Paul says that though we have faith to move mountains, without love it produces nothing of eternal value in our own lives. How sad to have an effective but empty ministry before God. There is, indeed, a place for suffering in God's will when rightly recognized. It is the royal road to a life and ministry of love and compassion.

Faith: Qualified by God's Will

It seems strange that some tragedies can begin in settings that appear so spiritual at their outset. A beloved brother in Christ shared with me a very sad and unfortunate experience which his family had recently undergone. It was his personal desire that the body of Christ might profit from the lessons they learned under very distressing circumstances. His wife had become involved in a prayer group where there had been an extreme emphasis on the unlimited results that faith can produce. How very much indeed our heavenly Father wants a family of faith in a world which is characterized by doubt and disbelief. Again, however, the deceiver will take truth and, through extremism, carry it over into error.

"If you ask anything in my name, I will do it . . ." became a basic universal promise which the group claimed almost without qualification. We need to understand that the name of Jesus is not a magic formula appended to the end of every prayer that guarantees its immediate answer. Rather, the name of God refers not only to His mighty power, but also to His changeless character and eternal purpose.

The will of God involves:

1. the right objectives
2. through the right method
3. with the right people
4. at the right time
5. in the right place
6. from the right motives

God's will brings all of the earthly, temporal, and physical factors into subjection to His heavenly, eternal, and spiritual purposes. His will involves His methods, timing, and motives—all elements which we can so easily overlook in our zeal for doing God's work our way.

The Setting for Serious Delusion

The prayer group had experienced a number of answers to prayer, and indeed the faith formulas appeared to be working without exception. Moreover, many prophecies in the name of the Lord seemingly were being fulfilled as faith reached out into yet greater possibilities. Demon powers were rebuked, and a strong sense of authority bordering on infallibility was recognized as the group grew "stronger" in the Lord.

Two serious needs developed. One involved the son of my friend and his wife, whose marriage to a prostitute was scheduled within the next couple of weeks. The other concerned the wife's sister-in-law who was terminally ill with cancer. The positive faith pattern was rigidly followed. A boy sat in proxy for the wayward son. An authoritative prophecy was given that the marriage would never take place. Much praise followed this declaration of faith.

A similar procedure was followed for the ailing sister-in-law. Again her healing was claimed and confessed on the sure Word of the Lord, and my friend's wife believed everything with all of her heart. There was no alternative but victory, because faith had triumphed over sin, Satan, demons, and death!

The wedding date arrived, and their son was married as had been originally planned. A few days later the sister-in-law died. Still, they held on in faith claiming her resurrection, but no such deliverance was forthcoming. In desperation, a disillusioned wife wrote for help to a noted faith teacher whose tapes and books they had used. His only reply was that he was not able to respond to personal letters. Her prayer partners informed her that the entire failure was due to her lack of faith, and then subjected her to a session for demonic deliverance, which left her in such a state of depression that she cursed God, and began entertaining thoughts of suicide.

After "blaspheming" God, she suffered the agony of feeling she had committed the unpardonable sin and was forever lost. Her poor husband could only love her, and pray for God's grace for her life. There was nothing else that could be done. All of the "methods" had failed.

The Father's Love Breaks Through

Her depression lasted for almost eight months with no

outward signs of improvement. Then one Sunday they chanced to visit a little church while on a short trip from home. Nothing occurred of a dramatic nature as far as outward demonstration was concerned. The minister preached a very simple sermon on the love of the Father in Christ Jesus. There can be great power in simplicity, especially when it involves the healing love of God. A light dawned in the darkness of her soul, and she began to recover from that day forward.

The truly tragic aspect of this entire story is that through a proper understanding of God's love, and His ultimate purpose, the entire experience could have been avoided. Sadly, the illustration we have used is not an isolated instance. Many of God's people are confused and disillusioned when they face misfortunes, accidents, and unexpected disappointments. They have been conditioned to think of God either as a cure-all, or when that fails, as a cruel and indifferent being whom they can neither understand nor love.

How very much we need to know the love of God and thereby trust the wisdom of His ways. How much better it is for us in our time of desperate need to readily, but humbly, come to our wise and loving heavenly Father and pray that His Spirit would direct us to the particular portion of His Word which He would have us claim for that moment. Sometimes He proposes to do an immediate and mighty miracle on our behalf. Other times our difficulty may be a symptom of a deeper need He wishes to reach either in our lives or within the body of Christ. His answer may involve a divine delay—as with Mary, Martha, and Lazarus—but never without divine purpose. Regardless of His methods, timing, or purpose, everything is always to be covered with His love. Herein is the sure ground for our faith and the promise for an abiding peace of mind.

6

It Will Be
Worth It All

The life of John the Baptist becomes a great blessing when we realize this mighty prophet of God faced times of doubt and concern as we all do. I am so glad that the grand heroes of faith in the Scriptures are not so saintly that we can't allow their experiences to become real lessons in life for us.

John was a very fascinating person. He was filled with the Spirit from his mother's womb. Because his parents Zechariah and Elizabeth were up in years, much of his young manhood must have been spent alone in the wilderness where the Scriptures simply state he lived the rather austere life of a prophet uniquely called of God. He wore clothes of camel's hair, girded by a leather belt. His diet consisted of locusts and wild honey— the latter apparently to assist the downing of the former.

He was not, however, unaware of the evils of his time and society. As someone poetically phrased it, "John was not afraid to speak forthrightly concerning the rote, rut, and rot of the religious systems of his day." In character he was as straight as an arrow, bold and fearless, but a man of great humility. He knew the voice of God and courageously spoke against the hypocrisy that existed at every level of life.

John also knew his calling and the boundaries of his ministry. His objective was to prepare the people for the coming of Christ—the promised Messiah. John referred to Jesus many times as the "Coming One" who was destined to establish God's kingdom on earth. But John's appreciation of Jesus ranged far beyond this, for as "the Lamb of God" he also recognized Him as the suffering Savior of the world. Still, his perspective was primarily that of an Old Testament prophet whose ministry was destined for a time of divine transition.

His concept of the kingdom probably contained both heavenly and earthly components. His baptism of repentance was intended to prepare men's hearts for a new work of God. This, in turn, was to be expressed by a change in the entire order of social structure. Justice and righteousness would yet rule and reign upon the earth as the Coming One would assume His royal commission in the kingdom of God.

The turning point in John's short ministry (some six months) came as he unselfishly proclaimed, "Behold the Lamb of God." From that time he confessed that Christ must increase, while he must decrease. More and more disciples then followed after Jesus, greatly to John's joy.

The Background for Doubt and Despair

The freedom of the man from the wilderness was short-lived, however, because his outspoken condemnation of Herod Antipas' illicit marriage to Herodias landed him in prison—the Castle of Machaerus—on the eastern shore of the Dead Sea. For a man of the open, wind-swept, sun-lit fields, actively stirring the hearts of the crowds in preparation for the Coming One, the dark and stuffy atmosphere of solitary confinement must have severely stressed the strong fibers of his soul. He had been a man with a free spirit, but now after months of waiting, he began to suffer the bondage of soul that doubt and frustration can bring.

Was Jesus really the Messiah? He had been so sure, the witness had been so strong within his spirit. Yet, here he had languished in prison for seven long months, while the very man he proclaimed would restore righteousness and justice through a fiery baptism was wining and dining with sinners.

Finally, in desperation, he sent two of his disciples to Jesus with a very pointed question, "Are you the One who is to come or should we look for another?" John had not given up hope that a Messiah would indeed come. This hope had been burned into his soul by both God's Word and God's Spirit, but he wondered whether Jesus was the Promised One. John's disciples faithfully conveyed his question personally to the Lord.

Christ: An Answer in Action

Christ's response to John's inquiry was most unusual, because He didn't say a word, but immediately proceeded to heal the sick, cast out demons, open blind eyes, cleanse the lepers, and preach the good news of the gospel to the poor. Then He told John's disciples to return and tell him what they had seen and heard.

There was a reason for this unusual action. Rather than trying to verbally persuade John's disciples concerning His true identity, He chose to actually fulfill the prophetic words of the Old Testament with which He knew John was familiar. Jesus realized such a witness would be honored by the Holy Spirit in John's heart and would provide all of the assurance such a man of faith would need.

Following the departure of John's disciples, Jesus made some very personal observations concerning John. We can be so very pleased and encouraged that all of His remarks were positive. He not once implied that John had started well but weakened in faith as his ministry came to a close. Rather He declared that there was none born of women who was greater than John. Yet Jesus explained a new order had come which was only seen by John from afar, as Moses had seen the promised land only from a distance. The new order involved a heavenly kingdom which would be ruled by the royal law of love in the hearts of men. Jesus Christ as the Son of man would be the Redeemer-brother through which the royal family of God would be formed. This revelation was only dimly perceived by John, and the time dimension in his mind had been telescoped to such a degree he assumed total fulfillment was going to be achieved immediately.

A Story With a Glorious Ending

However, upon being assured that Jesus truly was the Messiah—the promised Son of David, whose reign would be unto the ages—John was content to leave all the details in the hands of the King. John remained in prison for another nine months or so before he was beheaded. I fully believe, however, that during the remaining days, John's spirit was completely free, because earthly walls cannot contain the heavenly liberty which is produced by the Spirit of the living Christ!

John's martyrdom, rather than being a sad conclusion to a noble life, was truly more in the nature of a coronation. What a glorious welcome must have been his when as an honored son he entered into the presence of the God he had so faithfully served throughout his life. Surely all heaven joined in the celebration.

Offended by Jesus?

Jesus then said something else which is of supreme

importance to us in our day as we, too, wait for the fulfillment of God's kingdom, and seek in obedience to hasten the day of the King's appearing. The words are few, but powerful in meaning:

> Blessed is he who takes no offense at me. (Luke 7:23, RSV)

The key to this passage is the little word "offense." It is translated from the Greek noun *skandalon* and has a double derivation in meaning:

1. It was a term used to describe the bait-stick in a trap or snare, designed to tempt or entice an unwary victim.
2. It was also a word which referred to a stumbling block, which might act as an hindrance or barrier to one's progress.

Both thoughts convey the idea of limitation or hindrance to progress towards a given goal or objective. Jesus is saying to us that sometimes God's will is only partially in view; we see as only through a glass darkly. Therefore, if as John, we proceed to determine in our minds just precisely how, when, where, and through whom God is going to achieve His promised Word, we might be tempted (baited) and trapped by doubt and disappointment when things don't work out as we anticipated. Such spiritual confusion can cause us to stumble in our walk of faith and obedience. Ultimately the doubt is directed towards God's love for us and, as explained earlier, this sets off a chain reaction of negative attitudes and actions which become most grievous to both us and our heavenly Father.

Again we can see why it is so essential that our inner eye of faith be firmly fixed on the truth and power of God's love so the enemy has no ground upon which he can cause us to question the faithfulness of our heavenly Father.

Wanted: A Family for the Father

Paul really laid hold of—or perhaps we should say was gripped by—the ultimate and eternal purpose of God's great Father-heart. He is going to have a people, a beloved family, a royal priesthood, through whom the glorious life of His Son shall be forever expressed. In this our Father finds His heart desire, and we enter into the reward of ruling and reigning with our royal brother, Christ Jesus. It is from this heavenly perspective that in spite of earthly distresses and disappointments, Paul could triumphantly say:

> And since we are his children, we will share his treasures—for all God gives to his Son Jesus is now ours, too. But if we are to share his glory, we must also share his suffering. Yet what we suffer now is nothing compared to the glory He will give us later. (Rom. 8:17-18, TLB) So we do not lose heart. Though our outer nature is wasting away, our inner nature is being renewed every day. For this slight momentary affliction is preparing for us an eternal weight of glory beyond all comparison, because we look not to the things that are seen but to the things that are unseen; for the things that are seen are transient, but the things that are unseen are eternal. (2 Cor. 4:16-18, RSV)

Such a statement is far more than wishful sentiment, but gathers up the sweep of the ages into its scope, and brings us personally in touch with God's timeless purpose. We are here on earth for a heavenly reason. The events in time are all connected with eternal purpose. Everything is bent ultimately in one direction—the unchanging will of God.

It is the will of the Father to manifest His glory through a family of many sons and daughters whose lives have been perfected and purified through the fires of earthly circumstances. God is calling out a people who, because of His love for them, will trust and obey Him regardless.

> I have learned to be content, whatever the circumstances may be. I know now how to live when things are difficult, and I know how to live when things are prosperous. In general and in particular I have learned the secret of facing either plenty or poverty. I am ready for anything through the strength of the one who lives within me. (Phil. 4:11-13, Phillips)

The prevailing power which so possessed Paul's life rested securely on the sure ground of God's love:

> In all these things we win an overwhelming victory through him who has proved his love for us. I have become absolutely convinced that neither death nor life, neither messenger of Heaven nor monarch of earth, neither what happens today nor what may happen tomorrow, neither a power from on high nor a power from below, nor anything else in God's whole world has any power to separate us from the love of God in Christ Jesus our Lord! (Rom. 8:37-39, Phillips)

The power of God's love relentlessly moves us toward the perfection of divine purpose. Through Christ Jesus we are involved in that purpose, and thereby energized by that power. Though the outward circumstances of life may crumble, our frail bodies falter and fail, our minds weaken with age, and occasionally our emotions give way under pressure, still our spirits will ever remain strong and secure in Christ Jesus.

Such truth far from being unreachable "pie in the sky" is actually the very bread of our earthly existence. Jesus proved and pictured this power of God's loving purpose by His life, death, and resurrection. To know God's will brings both a strength and a set to our lives which cannot be shaken. However, for the soul already shattered by tragedy, doubt, and fear, it is still not too late, because there is healing and redeeming power for you from the loving heart of your heavenly Father.

You Have a Place in His Plan—Now and Hereafter

It has always been a great comfort to me to realize that God knows us better than we know ourselves. Furthermore, He has a plan and purpose for you. Even if you have seemingly wasted much of your life, He can still redeem it. Nothing is ever lost in God, and His plan for the rest of your life begins afresh every day.

The Psalmist must have personally been touched by this truth to have penned these encouraging words:

You made all the delicate, inner parts of my body, and knit them together in my mother's womb. Thank you for making me so wonderfully complex! It is amazing to think about. Your workmanship is marvelous—and how well I know it. You were there while I was being formed in utter seclusion! You saw me before I was born and scheduled each day of my life before I began to breathe. Every day was recorded in your Book! This is too glorious, too wonderful to believe! I can never be lost to your Spirit! I can never get away from my God! (Ps. 139:13-16, 6-7, TLB)

There is a quiet peace and confidence which comes in knowing we are the beloved children of our heavenly Father, and that His plan for our lives includes not only our lifetime as we know it, but also the hereafter as well. Actually the future life is even more important and wonderful than the present, because we will experience the freedom of our glorified bodies in an entirely new realm of existence. Yet, we will retain our individuality just as Scripture declares Jesus did in His glorified body:

As they were saying this, Jesus himself stood among them. But they were startled and frightened, and supposed that they saw a spirit. And he said to them, "Why are you troubled, and why do questionings rise in your hearts? See my hands and my feet, that it is I myself; handle me, and see; for a spirit has not flesh and bones as you see that I have." And while they still disbelieved for joy, and wondered, he said to them, "Have you anything here to eat?" They gave him a piece of broiled fish, and he took it and ate before them. (Luke 24:36-43, RSV)

But as of now we are still embodied by our temples of clay, and even the best of our earthly achievements family-wise will ultimately fade as the flowers in the field. But our heavenly Father is a master at family planning, and He envisions a household of faith and love that will live forever. His thoughts never stray from this objective. He is determined to fashion a people for His pleasure.

As a father pities his children, so the Lord pities those who fear him. For he knows our frame; he remembers that we are dust. As for man, his days are like grass; he flourishes like a flower of the field; for the wind passes over it, and it is gone, and its place knows it no more. But the steadfast love of the Lord is from everlasting to everlasting upon those who fear him, and his righteousness to children's children, to those who keep his covenant and remember to do his commandments. (Ps. 103:13-18, RSV)

The word pity is derived from the Hebrew word *racham*. It is a very weak translation, because the meaning in the original language has a far more powerful and positive intent. One of its root words means to fondle or caress. A noun of the same family refers to the womb—a place of protection, nourishment, and development. The idea involves a feeling of compassion whereby God desires to lovingly hold and shape our earthly lives for His heavenly purpose.

Somewhere along this same line I remember John Wright Follette, a godly teacher of years past, remarking that it did his "dust" so much good just to know God remembers our origin, and is acquainted with our limitations. As a loving Father, He desires to fashion our lives into something beautiful for our good and His everlasting glory.

Clay in the Potter's Hand

This thought is carried over into Isaiah's poetic prophecy concerning God's faithfulness to perfect His people as they would willingly submit to the loving work of His hand:

Yet, O Lord, thou art our Father; we are the clay,

and thou art our potter; we are all the work of thy hand. (Is. 64:8, RSV)

For emphasis we could chart this verse as follows:

Thou	**We**
Father	Clay
Potter	Handwork

The fragile clay of our lives is pictured as resting securely in the hands of our faithful Father who, as the Divine Potter, skillfully shapes our vital dust into vessels of honor designed to contain the glory of Christ's image. As previously mentioned, for those who love God and are called according to His purpose, all things are working together for good (Rom. 8:28). It is comforting to know that the hands of our heavenly Father are fashioning and forming (working together) every detail of our daily lives in keeping with His divine design.

For we are his workmanship, created in Christ Jesus for good works, which God prepared beforehand, that we should walk in them. (Eph. 2:10, RSV)

The potter of that day was careful to use clay which was both pure and finely worked by treading. Impurities or coarse particles would ultimately spoil the final product. When moistened to the proper consistency, the clay was thrown on the wheel where the hands of the potter carefully controlled both the inside and outside dimensions of the intended vessel. After drying and firing, the vessel was sufficiently hardened and could be beautifully decorated and glazed.

The treading, shaping, and firing processes which God uses in perfecting our lives are the daily circumstances of our earthly existence. Nothing is ever wasted or worthless if placed in the hand of our Father. Moreover, much of what He is doing deep within our lives is unseen at the outset, but the outcome is clearly in view in the vision of God. Again His perspective goes beyond the limited span of our lifetime on earth, and includes the ages to come. God's will is a process which does not stop with death. We need to be conditioned to this larger horizon or we will ever be measuring things by a short and faulty yardstick.

The Loving Hands of a Faithful Father

The hands of God can protect, correct, and direct our lives—and those of our loved ones—if we will but make that commitment in faith to His sure words of hope and love. The Lord once brought me up short with the challenge: "Why do you persist in seeing your children in the hands of the devil, rather than in the hands of their faithful Shepherd?" I then realized that in my mind I had been imagining all of the evils of our present age as being ultimately more powerful than the timeless love of God. Ultimately, God's love will prevail. It has the persistent power to convict, forgive, redeem, and restore. This should be our stand now before God, as it will be on that day when we see Him face to face.

A mother once shared a most encouraging insight which confirms and extends this divine truth. Her wayward son had raised and dashed her hopes so many times that she was on the verge of collapse. She finally saw the privilege and responsibility of standing with God and the answer, rather than with her son and the problem. She totally released her boy in the hands of her wise and loving heavenly Father. After all, she had dedicated her boy to God, and in that sense he was His son, too. There were further disappointments, but each time she faithfully confessed that this was something else God would use to ultimately bring her boy back to himself. It took some years, but the miracle did occur, and now this mother can sympathetically, but faithfully minister hope to others in similar situations.

To turn a matter over to God does not mean we no longer have a loving, prayerful concern, but now the primary responsibility rests with God, not us. We may not see the results outwardly in our lifetime or perhaps theirs, but we can stand firm in our faith—even for divine accomplishments which occur during the transitional moments between life and death. God's work within the spirit of man is not limited to the clinically conscious mind, as many testimonies under such circumstances confirm. Our responsibility is to faithfully maintain our confession as long as we have breath—regardless of outward events. In this we share our faith with those of ages past who believed what they had not yet seen.

> All these whom we have mentioned maintained their faith but died without actually receiving God's promises, though they had seen them in the distance, had hailed them as true and were quite convinced of their reality. (Heb. 11:13, Phillips)

Christ: The Father's Only Answer

A middle-aged mother who had just recently found the Lord as her Savior requested the privilege of being filled with the Holy Spirit that she might have the consolation and strength which the Blessed Comforter brings. Her daughter had recently committed suicide and she was facing this personal tragedy as best she could.

She confided in me that she had found real comfort from some of her friends who were involved with spiritualism and seances. Her daughter had been contacted on the other side and had requested that her mother be informed that she was at peace—all was well—and she was not to worry or be in grief.

My heart dropped as I listened to these false words of comfort devilishly designed to deceive a baby in Christ during her personal hour of bereavement. One feels very helpless at such a time, and the wise and loving ministry of the Holy Spirit is most welcome. I knew God must have a better answer, and proceeded to tell her so after warning her concerning the dangers of demonic deception. She immediately and gratefully received my admonition, and then waited for the better answer that God had for her.

I knew our heavenly Father had made full provision for His beloved children in Christ Jesus, so this seemed a wise and safe place to begin. Following the next thought that came to my mind, and claiming it to be of the Lord, I inquired if she had been praying for her daughter prior to this tragedy, and had committed her in faith into the hands of Jesus as her Good Shepherd. She assured me that she had faithfully and repeatedly made this her confession. Proceeding along the same lines of inspiration, I then suggested that she leave her there—in the hands of Jesus—because He was someone she could confidently trust without fear or deception or disappointment.

She gratefully received that word, and entered into the joy and peace of inspired prayer and praise as we led her on into the beautiful experience of Holy Spirit baptism. The loving, gracious witness of God's Spirit assured us both that there are mysteries in the celestial realm that we can confidently give to the care and keeping of our loving heavenly Father.

Father Wants to Make It Up to You—in Heaven

In all that we have shared thus far, we discover that

although God's ultimate purpose in redemption is yet to be completed, there are many aspects of that redemption which are provided for us while the process of the Father's will is being fulfilled. God truly wants to make it up to us for the pain, tragedy, and misfortune which falls the lot of both Christian and non-Christian. Again we are not spared all of the adversities of life, but they all can be utilized in God's divine plan for us now and hereafter.

Some of our rewards relate to the wonderful world of the coming age of Christ's kingdom. To rule and reign with Christ is far more than just sitting behind golden thrones with jeweled scepters in our hands. I feel it includes the realms of nature which were never really brought into dominion by man as was his original commission. Scientific progress to date has been phenomenal, but it has also caused more problems than it has solved. The total harmony of life and nature as God anticipated it to be still remains beyond man's reach. Social advances are again commendable, but no real answer can come for the ills of society until the spiritual sickness in man's soul is cured. But under Christ's royal rule of love what exciting possibilities exist! Energies directed towards selfish profit and protection will be rechanneled into discovering God's laws of universal harmony and peace. In God's grace we shall participate in extending His divine order into every dimension of the universe, and this takes us beyond all of the boundaries of conceptual thought. Each new wonder will become a window which will bring us into profound worship and praise.

Most wonderful of all will be the reality of the heavenly realm wherein our personal relationship with God will surpass any earthly reference we have. A friend of mine once had a vision of heaven, and he tried to explain something of its beauty and glory. Everything was an expression of praise and worship to God by its very nature and being.

The trees, birds, and animals all were giving glory to Jesus Christ through their very existence. Peace ruled supreme. Everything was in divine harmony with everything else. There was no discord or disorder at any level. Even the colors were spiritually alive. As his vision dimmed, he said the colors of earth—even the brightest—seemed dull and lifeless in comparison.

And we now are being prepared to find our place in that celestial world. But not all positions are alike. My friend saw people as goblets—all were filled to overflowing—but the capacity of the goblets varied to a considerable degree. The interpretation is obvious, our capacity to experience the glorious life of Jesus is in part at least being determined by our life relationship with Him now—here on earth!

Father Wants to Make It Up to You—Now!

But not all of our rewards are relegated to the hereafter. The various Scriptures and illustrations we have used indicate there are several ways which God wants to compensate us for our suffering while we complete our life here on earth. Perhaps we have missed something which is waiting to be recognized and experienced just because we were unaware of God's gracious desire to provide for us in the present.

We can summarize these expectations for divine compensation as follows:

1. *A personal disclosure of himself*
   It is during times or under conditions of personal disappointment that we should look for God to reveal something special to us concerning himself. Often it is during adversity that we really come to know the true nature of the Father, Son, and Holy Spirit in a warm, loving, living, personal way. May we learn to

wait upon Him for the awareness of His presence, because He is waiting for us.

2. *A realization of God's family*
   Many times it is only through affliction that we truly come to know and appreciate our brothers and sisters (and mothers and fathers) in the Lord. Their ministry of love and wisdom in the Holy Spirit not only heals and restores us personally, but vitally relates us to one another. Remember there is relationship in the image of God. "Let us make man in *our* image! How very much we need each other. The love of our brothers and sisters is a precious gift from God.

3. *A ministry to others*
   Only those who themselves have suffered the fires of affliction can minister with love, compassion, sympathy, and empathy—yet with faith, force, and conviction to others in their time of adversity. There is an intercessory ministry that can emerge from our valley experiences that enables us to relate to others—and even more important, for them to relate to us—in their time of need. We truly can minister the consolation and comfort of God, for we have experienced it ourselves. Look for such opportunities, because the Father is seeking for those who will bring healing to His suffering sons and daughters. Furthermore, we don't have to wait until we have gone through our valley to help another, not if we have found Jesus there ourselves!

4. *A ministry to God*
   At first this may seem an unexpected possibility when we ourselves are in need. But there is

nothing more precious to God than our praise during affliction. Not praise for what the devil has done, but praise for the redeeming power of our loving heavenly Father. What He does not protect us from, He will perfect us through. There is indeed a special blessing for those who do not become offended in God during adversity. Furthermore, we become a special blessing to Him!

Let me now share with you one more illustration from life for it seems such a fitting conclusion for the theme of this chapter.

Something Supremely Precious to Our Heavenly Father

Several years ago a friend of ours went to her doctor over the weekend for a special examination because a suspicious lump had suddenly developed. She hadn't bothered her husband concerning the matter because he was scheduled to be away over the weekend, and she had restfully committed everything to the Lord.

After the biopsy was taken and diagnosed, her doctor informed her that he had scheduled her the next Monday for a radical mastectomy. When her husband returned home they agreed in prayer with their local prayer community that everything was in the hands of God, their heavenly Father, and they trusted Him to provide for her according to His will. They believed in and had experienced God's healing power in the past, so they were confident that the Lord would graciously respond as He knew best for all concerned. They rested in His peace.

Monday's surgery was completed as scheduled. The physical healing which they had earnestly prayed for in faith had not occurred. But another healing did. Not only was her

136

recovery remarkably rapid, there was absolutely no post-surgical depression. It was only a matter of weeks before they joyfully and peacefully went to Israel for ministry which had been planned before the unexpected surgery occurred. The greater blessing, however, was yet to come.

Some mutual friends of ours who have a beautiful prophetic ministry visited with them while on a trip in the area. The events of the past months were being shared when the Holy Spirit brought forth a most remarkable prophecy. With great feeling the heavenly Father expressed His special love for this His dearest daughter during her time of trial and affliction. Furthermore, she was assured that her faith in God, which took her through without doubt or question, was to Him supremely precious. She had indeed ministered to the Lord by her simple faith in God's loving care regardless of the outcome in the natural. Her pain and physical loss were more than compensated for by her heavenly Father's loving response.

Indeed, she had entered into a wiser and more loving relationship with God; she personally experienced the care and comfort which can only come from the faith and love of our brothers and sisters in Christ. She also received a much greater ministry of faith and compassion for the afflicted in the family of God, and most of all she had broken the alabaster box of faith, hope, and love at the feet of Jesus. One can almost hear the heavenly Father say:

> You are a beloved daughter in whom I am well pleased; you are most precious in my sight. Tell my people that I love them, tell them that I care.